The
Friday Noon
Poetry Club

POETRY

UNDER

THE

STARS

MOORE PUBLISHING COMPANY
DURHAM, NORTH CAROLINA 27705

Copyright © 1979 by Moore Publishing Company,
P. O. Box 3036, Durham, North Carolina 27705

Library of Congress Catalog Number: 79-65627
ISBN: 0-87716-106-2

Printed in the United States of America.

ACKNOWLEDGMENTS

Acknowledgment is made to the following for permission to reprint copyrighted materials. Special acknowledgment is also extended to Sam Ragan for his efforts in the capacity of consulting editor for this anthology.

"the first time i felt," by Nina A. Wicker. Copyright ©1979 by the *Cairn*. Reprinted with permission.

"Dreams," by Brenda Loy Williamson-Pratt. Reprinted with permission of *Carolina Woman*, May 1979.

"Salome" and "Sarah, the Beloved Wife," by Kate Kelly Thomas. Copyright ©1978 by the *Christian Poetry Journal*. Reprinted with permission.

"Coming Out," by Shelby Stephenson. First printed in *Commonweal*.

"The Second Season," by Mitchell Forrest Lyman. First printed in *The Crucible*.

"God's Eye," by Betty Bolton. Reprinted with permission. First printed in *Sixty North Carolina Poets*, East Carolina Poetry Forum Series, no. 14, 1974.

"Meteor Man," by Margaret Boothe Baddour. First printed in the *International Poetry Review*, Fall 1975. Reprinted with permission.

"Carolina" and "Giraffe," by Calvin Atwood, from *Squadron of Roses*. Copyright ©1978 by Moore Publishing Company.

"The Awakening" and "Reflections While Serving as a Judge for the Selection of the Cheerleaders," by Ellen Turlington Johnston-Hale, from *We Don't Do Nothin' in Here*. Copyright ©1976 by Moore Publishing Company.

"Archaic Grace" and "Nightwatch," by Sallie Nixon, from *Second Grace*. Copyright ©1977 by Moore Publishing Company.

CONTENTS

POETRY UNDER THE STARS: From Inner Spaces

POETRY UNDER THE STARS

PUBLISHER'S NOTE

Poetry Under the Stars is a book by beginning poets, or at least poets who are beginning to publish. It has arisen from the Friday Noon Poets who meet for lunch/readings every Friday at the Red Baron Restaurant whose atmosphere is hospitable to poets and whose location at the edge of Chapel Hill is convenient to area poets most of whom come from Durham, Raleigh, Greensboro, Burlington, Sanford, and Southern Pines. In North Carolina where poets abound such an area includes a fair number of these creative people. One of these poets, Lois Holt, expresses the spirit of the group in her poem, "For All the Red Barons": Whatever this is . . . / A chapter, paragraph, / a simple phrase / one note from a symphony / a dab from the painter's brush; / it's enough . . . / to lean against / the tip of one finger to touch.

The area also includes the University of North Carolina's Planetarium and its very able director, Anthony Francis Jenzano, Sr., who appreciates the value of poetry in a perspective that includes the awe-inspiring audiovisual effects afforded by his institution. The first reading at the Planetarium was arranged through the combined efforts of Mr. Jenzano and Lois Holt, a poet included in this anthology. It was highly successful as a community exposition and demand for its continuance was immediately forthcoming. Subsequent readings have already been scheduled as an ongoing series and are planned for other planetariums.

Poetry Under the Stars takes its title from this first-of-its-kind event and a separate section appears in the book to include these reading poets as well as those included in the general anthology.

The reader will find a full and satisfying range of poetry in this volume. Since the poet is not alone in viewing life, discernments are not always his/her own but may be the spirit or muse passing along perceptions. Likely almost everyone is capable of poetic expressions, needs only to experience and to relate that wellspring of creativity. An example is a personal experience that involved two remarkable women whom I met during a recent trip on which there was an audience with the Pope and professional activity in a hospital in India. Impressed and inspired was I; and the words easily came. Muse, Spirit, and God were speaking. I merely listened and wrote.

TERESA

Near the Pope she sat,
Nearer yet to me
As if I were to know
Of truth and beauty,

That I might recognize
Service seniority
And be not content
With my juniority.

Mother of Calcutta,
Of poor and dying fame,
Great servant of God
Teresa was her name.

The audience knew her well
Tiny—taller than the rest
And Princes kissed the hand
Of Sister Teresa, the blessed.

REBEKAH

No Sunnybrook Farm, Rebekah
Rather a theater of life,
This work of God you have chosen.
I watch as you go a 'healing
Applying your skill swift and sure.
I see you as teacher, preacher;
Yet I see the child, woman too,
And always the Christian comes through.
Tend God's children now, Rebekah,
And let your beauty so increase
That all India, yea the world
Will know you as great physician
Of body and soul and of God.

We who are included in *Poetry Under the Stars* welcome comments, critical or otherwise, on our poetry. It is hoped that each contributor may one day publish an individual volume and response by readers of this anthology may expedite such a publication. Thus far, although appearing in literary magazines and/or newspaper columns, none of the poets contributing to the general anthology has published a book of poetry. It is only a matter of time and a matter of who will be first.

Eugene V. Grace
Publisher

Poetry Under the Stars:

The Reading

CONTRIBUTING POETS

Calvin Atwood
An assistant dean in the graduate school at the University of North Carolina, Mr. Atwood merges strength and tenderness in his poetry, which touches everyone. He is the author of a recently published volume of poetry, *A Squadron of Roses.*

Margaret Boothe Baddour
President of the North Carolina Poetry Society and past director of the Goldsboro Community Arts Council, Mrs. Baddour has led poetry workshops and has given readings all over North Carolina. Her poems have been featured in several magazines.

Eugene V. Grace
Dr. Grace, a practicing ophthalmologist in Durham and the founder of Moore Publishing Company, attended UCLA before obtaining his M.D. at the University of Michigan.

Sara Hunter
Dr. Hunter was a medical and textbook editor and science writer before earning her Ph.D. in clinical psychology at the University of Minnesota in 1974. She came to Chapel Hill as an assistant professor of psychology and has a small private practice.

Ellen Turlington Johnston-Hale
An author of two books, *So What Happened To You?* and *We Don't Do Nothin' in Here!,* Mrs. Johnston-Hale is currently serving as second vice-president of the North Carolina Poetry Society and is Poet-in-the-Schools in North Carolina.

Agnes McDonald
A resident of Raleigh and a professor in the English Department of North Carolina State University, Ms. McDonald's longtime interest in poetry has led to her active participation in and support of the North Carolina Poetry Society.

Sallie Nixon
A Phi Beta Kappa graduate of the University of Nebraska and the recipient of numerous awards for creative writing, Mrs. Nixon has

been a poet for 20 years. She is past president of the North Carolina Poetry Society and is the author of *Second Grace*, a volume of poetry.

Stan Smith

A psychotherapist and problem-solving consultant in Chapel Hill, Mr. Smith spent his growing-up years in South Africa and Virginia. He is father, husband, friend, and his interests include cooking, chess, and writing poetry.

Mary C. Snotherly

The 1979 membership chairman for the North Carolina Poetry Society, Ms. Snotherly was the featured winner in the 1978 publication of the Society's *Award Winning Poems*. An employee of Eastern Airlines, she lives in Raleigh.

Shelby Stephenson

Pembroke State University professor in the Department of Communicative Arts, Mr. Stephenson is a member of the North Carolina Poetry Society and an enthusiastic leader of regional workshops across the state.

GIRAFFE (for Martha—not quite to teens)

I think it's very funny that you call me "Giraffe";
It's kind of a spiffy name
And tells me that I'm not exactly the same
As other animals, and I don't want to be.

Do you call me that because of my long neck,
Or because of my strange ears
Which behave badly sometimes except when they want to hear
Lovely, small people like you who smile with their toes.

The orange giraffe you made for me I broke,
Like I break most everything,
But even the pieces sing,
And I am keeping them to see if they will grow back together again.

If I were a giraffe, I'd elongate my neck
And stretch longingly over the pines,
Over all time-space lines
To see if you're joshing someone—see what you're up to.

Did you know there's a constellation named for giraffes?
A tall brave gang of stars,
Shines bright on hurts and scars,
And might just keep an eye on us—keep us friends.

Calvin Atwood

CAROLINA

Towered over by green pines,
showered with rain
and needles of the pines,
greened by the everlasting green
of the Carolina hills;
whatever is Irish in me
keens for the never-weaning
from these life-green days,
from these drawling, slow words,
and this clock that crawls:

Don't never turn me loose.

Calvin Atwood

METEOR MAN

He was a lone star.
He hurtled east from the promised land
hit these thirteen colonies
like a boiling comet
his blue eyes
firing shrapnel bits of the universe.

He was also a rich brown bottle of tonic
a medicine show man from the prairie.

He was Rudyard Kipling
in the jungles of India and the Philippines.
Years after the war
he spoke highly of the Maharaja of Birdwan—
perhaps he really knew him.

For me he was vast
in the sky blue uniform.
Why one long-boned hand
could cover my whole small back.

And when I found myself
a tiny meteoric fragment of the man
I knew I could mold earths
in my hands
send suns twinkling from my feet.

Margaret Boothe Baddour

AND WE WERE GOD

Before heaven and earth
there was you and me
and we
were GOD.

And we plucked bits
of skin to make the earth
in our own image
and it wasn't all pretty
but what was pretty
was breathtaking.
And we laughed long and hard
at our creation.

Now the earth
wears our clothes
heaves when we speak
or twitch or cry.
All lines are defined
by my cheek bones
and winds
caused by your every breath.
Our eyes water the fountains
our heat bakes all the crops.

But when the wretched earth rebels
when we meet, churning,
in our own wind tunnel
the victims of our own creation
then I remind you of our power.
That's when we laugh again
and we laugh most always.

Margaret Boothe Baddour

THEY STEPPED ON OUR MOON TODAY

They stepped on our moon today.
Just a small step called giant
For mankind they say they stepped.
Still our moon pulls ocean tides
And mirrors love to lovers.
Changing still from waxing smile,
It rounds to harvest fullness.
Unmoved, stark on winter's sky,
Golden over horizon's shoulder,
Soft and warm on Summer's night,
Satellite love in springtime,
Our moon still beams our dreams
Of love and night-time wonder.

Eugene V. Grace

OUT HERE WHERE NOTHING BARS

Out here where nothing bars
My view of sky and stars,
Beyond the voice of friends
Where even their earth ends,
The stars stretch endlessly
Beyond where eye can see,
Their lights lit long ago
Longer than mind can know
Out here, at night, alone
World, God and I are one.

Eugene V. Grace

WHAT DIES ON ROADS

Soon I will be a dead animal,
huddled in fur on the road,
flattened tire by tire,
a stain that rains away,
and no one to know any more
the dog-pain place where I lay.
Squirrel-heart, rabbit-flight,
cat-heat longing:
What dies on roads
is what I am.

Sara Hunter

THE FINEST MADNESS

Lycanthropy, elegant insanity,
the delusion of wolfhood,
superior madness:
   better than unpersonment,
   better than accusing voices,
   better than guilt pawing the gut,
   better than freezing sadness:
flamboyance of howling and hair,
moon-called, running the night,
no werewolf but wolf throughout!

Sara Hunter

REFLECTIONS WHILE SERVING
AS A JUDGE
FOR THE SELECTION OF THE CHEERLEADERS

The rating sheets place
    COORDINATION first.
Then VOICE —
is it "resonant" and "loud"?
    ENTHUSIASM and VITALITY
    SMILE. POSTURE. POISE.
How will she look
    leading cheers before the crowd?
TWO JUMPS required.
ONE CARTWHEEL and ONE SPLIT.
Then, at least one INDIVIDUAL STUNT,
    (or more, if she sees fit).
We, the judges, who decide the fate
    of the young girls spinning shiny dreams,
    sit here stiffly in straight chairs and wait,
    scanning the evaluation sheets.
With a flick-flick of a ballpoint pen,
    five points here, three there,
    check-check, check-check,
    we determine who will make the team.

Now they come — in threes,
    tiny waists and pretty dimpled knees;
    swishing, flirty hips and dimpled smiles,
    swishing, shiny, flowing hair.

Give at least twelve points here
    for the bouncy, bubbly blond,
    smooth and agile — check.
    Eight points for the vibrant voice. Check.
    VITALITY? Oh yes! Oh my yes! Give her ten.
The redhead, more than graciously endowed . . .
    would she please the crowd?
    Oh MY yes! Yes *indeed* she would!
    Give here nine for posture. POISE? Good!

The short brunette does back bends,
    rolling up into a limber ball,

      doing somersaults along the floor.
         Check-Check. Check-check.

Pretty, graceful, mobile — one and all;
      swishy, slender, sassy — every one,
      each a XEROX of the one before.

Three groups down; two more groups to go.

There she is.
      A skinny, floppy, ragdoll of a girl;
      No chest, no waist, no hips to swish,
       her bony legs — parentheses;
       the brown hair limply listless, scraggly thin,
       the mouth — thin-lipped, set straight;
       scared, dull eyes,
       the kind that never really reach another's,
       but in shyness always turn away.
      She moves — a scarecrow among the others,
       duck-footed, hesitant.
      The others raise the left hand; she — the right.
      Turn a CARTWHEEL? Do a SPLIT? She can't.
      Her turn to lead the cheer.
          VOICE?
      How many points can you give for that pinched, tiny wail,
       strangely empty, hollow?
          COORDINATION?
      When she jumps, her legs don't want to follow
       the rest of her.
      Her arms — two sticks that flail,
       tiny windmills fanning at the air.

How many points?

You scan the sheet . . .
      Nothing allowed for courage here;
      not a check allowed
      for fighting out against the odds,
      for trying, amid astonished stares,
       of pretty, lithesome sprites.
      No points given here for challenging the gods,

who, doling out their gifts,
presented her a hand of losing cards.
No points given here for one who has
no beauty and no skill; yet, unawares,
she struggles.
And 'though she *has* to know she can't . . .
she *dares*.

Ellen Turlington Johnston-Hale

THE AWAKENING

We had this talent show.
We called it "Together."
　And it *was*.
We had songs
　and skits,
　drama, dance, and more.
　HITS!
And a BIG band with vocalists
　who handsomely wore
　sleek scarlet suits
with tight satin pants.
　TOGETHER!
　We got it ON!

We carefully screened all the acts,
　so they'd be "top drawer,"
　and tasteful,
　and nothing would get out of hand.

We screened all the acts . . . except one.
This young lady, who tried out with a young man
　for the Dance Contest part of the show,
　was VERY good.
She had the agiles,
　and the mobiles,
　and all the moves a dancer should.
She could do the limbo . . .
　I mean — she could make her whole *body*
　parallel to her knees, you know,
　and walk around that way.
　Incredible!
At the last minute before we drew up the program,
　she asked could she do a "Creative Dance,"
　　solo.
I said, "O.K."
It didn't seem to be taking a chance,
　for she was a lovely young lady,
　everyone said so.
　Quiet. Demure. Shy.

(They told me her mother was *very* strict with her,
  which explained why
  she was so demure . . . and quiet . . . and shy.)

Her dance came on half-way through.
I missed the start of it.
  (I was out in the hall, in fact,
  when she commenced her act).

I returned to the wings
  and heard whistles and wolf-calls and things
  that people don't usually *do* for a "Creative Dance,"
  nor for any part of it . . .
  not even when it's very *good*.
The young men backstage were watching,
  and choking in short, gaspy pants,
  "I can't take much more!,"
  as they shoved one another aside, so they *could*.

I, too, looked out from back there.
In my first frozen glance,
I perceived wriggling, writhing, contorting HER,
  making moves that *I* never knew *were*!

One trembling young man wheezed weakly,
  "She shouldn't be doing THAT . . . *should* she?"

    I nodded — mutely,
    feeling the same thing . . . acutely.

Indeed, this was no "*Creative* Dance."
Our prim young *prima donna* was doing a DIRTY dance.
And that captive audience: those mothers —
  not hers, but others,
  and nice little sisters and brothers,
  were getting a whole LOT more
  than they bargained for!
(Thank goodness, HER mom wasn't there.
  She'd not have considered it funnery.
  She'd have got that poor girl to the nearest nunnery.)

Now, here's some advice, and it's sage:
All ye talent show sponsors, BEWARE
  of quiet young shy Innocence.
For, bathed in the spotlight's glare,
  beyond Mama's hovering care,
  finding its place in the sun
  up on that glittering stage —
  before God and everyone —
  it bumps and grinds and lets down its hair . . .
  and relentlessly comes of age!

Ellen Turlington Johnston-Hale

TO MY FATHER, THAT SUMMER

Forgetting early, remembering
late at the closing point, turning of my mind's shutter,
memory clicks.
Going back to green that moist tobacco town
(something there was I did not know it you),
I daily rang the tree-lashed park, circled my hours,
wore a three-stoned ring, my children.

Your woman child, ringing my fractured circle,
I wound it to the wound we bled between us. Then we,
talking like friends, then we, strolling the rose-
drenched evening of a summer not like any other,
then we, closing the circle of our love before death,
father of us both, shut down our rose-green park,
called in our ball.

Agnes McDonald

ASHLAND 1960

It was standing, the shadow-slanting poor man's brick-
covered repeat of houses we had seen
in our roams on roads edged by woods
and fenced by abandonment.
Neglect had reared it proud out of spring house
and cistern mound it grew
out of pity into tree nestles where squirrels
bombed its tin roof with disdain.
We took sides under blankets, under rain that ground its teeth
pointed into our black evenings starred and baying
over ridges we saw only in moonlight.
We stood in our simple bodies lighted by fires of our making,
saw us in perilous lanterns lively and loving,
touching from distances of frost fields and fox runs
to the red-coal center of our breath.

Agnes McDonald

TO ARCHAIC GRACE

Alcman knew the speech of birds and found
His own by listening to partridges. He heard
The seasons come, and his ear received the word
Of river, wave, and rock. To such he bound
His lines while the purpling sea curved in around
Him, and the long-stretched wing of ocean bird
With dappled neck flashed overhead and swirled
His waiting mind with ancient tunes of sound.
We awake to sing: Sappho rejected as unseemly
Lamentation in the house of those who serve
The Muses. She too survives with tender line
Held out line flowers in the hand. Poetry,
Come gentle; leave unwound no pressing nerve;
Praise the world's dark words; praise mine.

Sallie Nixon

NIGHTWATCH

All of what I must in this starry chorus
know, I do, and take in with certainty the
sharp of snow-night breath, and the ache of crystal
silences breaking.

Sallie Nixon

MOON

She is a stripper,
  Excruciatingly slow,
    Revealed shade by shade.
They say that when she is fully exposed
Males go mad follow her always,
Addicted lunatics.

Father heaves tidal heartbeats.
The constant lover waits while the strobe
Whites her out.
He thrusts mountains against seams.

One day, the San Andreas fault
  Will snap sending
    California semen to make that futile leap.

Father's tongue lolling, leering.
No newspaper, raincoat, or cap
To cover that total lunge

Till space, the bouncer,
Will set him in his seat again.

Father will lick his lips,
Let the goosebumps go,
Till she circles round again.

Stan Smith

GOLEM COUPLE

They used to call you two the royal family,
First cousins, spouses, a couple woven into a
Single shawl of genes, traditions, and spirit.
When cancer clawed away her breasts, did a pincer
Snatch the thread of your soul along with her life?
Did cancer, scuttling off, leave you a Golem?

Your second wife, smelling of schmaltz, salt, and schtettle
Speaks Yiddish gibberish to herself in the kitchen,
Nodding like an ancient cabbalist computing the coming full moon
While boiling fish falls from the bones
Like rotted flesh of corpses killed by cossacks.

Together you fend off exorcisms of wonder-working rabbis.
The prayers of your family float over you.
You sink in the sludge of ghetto cesspools,
Crabs scavenging the souls of the lost, the beaten,
And the gutless, my grandfather, my Golem.

Stan Smith

THESE MEXICANOS

they come
to go,
these Mexicanos,
to airports.

they are lean
and hard,
with flashing teeth
and smiling eyes
that question words.
their bodies
supple
from stretching
for cherries,
stooping for strawberries,
laboring long,
sleeping Spartan-hard.

they come
to go.
they bring
their suitcase-boxes,
wound with rope,
locked tight in knots.
they buy tickets
with crumpled
twenty-dollar bills,
and fives and ones,
and two dollars
in warm coins.

Mary C. Snotherly

WIND IN THE CATACOMBS

It was cold
as we descended
the catacombs
Stone cold.
The wind was black
having come so far
from the deep wound
Traveled so long
the everlasting maze
Having run fumbling fingers
over miles of craggy walls
Missing no nook
no single corridor.
Crashing headlong
the bolted doors
in bottled rage
Retracing steps
Pacing cages.
Tapping white canes
across cavern floors
Stumbling over fallen rock
Sighing
Struggling up again.
Clawing, groping
Going nowhere
finding nothing
Wailing the songs
of lost souls.
The wind in the catacombs
tireless and tired
Blindly searching
for the beginning
or the end
Finding us
Blocking the way
to the final light.

Mary C. Snotherly

EARS AND WINGS

When I was born
my ears were so big
Daddy put me on the top doorstep
he said
to see if I would fly.
Now I am drunk in a flutter of wings
and my sparse hair tickles
like new bird stubble.
Sparrows fly through my head
twelve out of twenty-four,
through one ear and out the other.
And they warble as they fly.
Sometimes the sun shines
deep in my sleep,
those birds again,
pitching on the top doorstep.

Shelby Stephenson

COMING OUT

The hour is a lovely tale,
Heaven, a flight of quail,
Prayer, a patient man.

Redweeds stay the storm in the branch,
Sanded lines where trickles run nowhere
And bottom is ashen as the old house,
Three rooms coming together
Freed from foundations
On winds over the eastern shore.

I turn through a door.
Ashes sit in the hearth.
Smoke blooms like roses.

A turning is in this hollow.
I shut my eyes, etch a tree in an orchard of walnuts.
A swing blows in the windhead of spring.

I wander beside the stream,
Roll in warm beds of grass,
Turn the tenderest stems to buds.

My swim is a plunge: the rope-swing moves.
How quiet the startled fish leap
In the grandeur of the water, creeping braids
From me to a tumble of springs
Where lily-pads slip
And the garden is bird-full and rich-throated.

I lie down in breezeless air,
Blow an owl's song
With a fist I shape into a horn,
My fingers closing shut over hand and mouth.
Gently lifting, the sound floats between my eyes.

A sparrow waves on the sill, worm-pleased,
Tail ruffled back toward beak
Curving light from the widening green.

Running into the grass
I gather a boat in my arms
And the frail stars
Cover my body like a net.
I drink good nectar in soft leaves
I cup to hold the juices.

A thrush comes out of the deep.
With stars containing my past journeys
I sit along ditches on hills
That remind me of home,
Move through lanes, backlots, paths to sawmills—
Measure the warm distance.

Shelby Stephenson

Poetry Under the Stars:

From Inner Spaces

BETTY BOLTON

Elizabeth Grier Bolton was born in Charlotte, North Carolina, and grew up in Georgia. She has lived for many years in Chapel Hill, North Carolina and holds degrees from the University of North Carolina and Teachers College, Columbia University. Miss Bolton has been an English teacher and librarian and in 1978 retired after nineteen years as librarian in the Louis Round Wilson Library of the University of North Carolina. She is a member of the North Carolina Poetry Society, Friends of the University of North Carolina Library, Friday Noon Poetry Club, and University Baptist Church.

A WISH

What comfort in March
there must be
to break forth green
like a tree.

Or push out buds
and have the power
to burst into blossom
like a flower.

Or as a bird
know how to share
great joy, and fling
a song upon the air.

I wish that I could
bud or leaf or sing
to express the way
I feel in spring.

DEAD SQUIRREL

Stiff and still in the street,
his arched tail now
limp and straight,
a pancake squirrel

Dries on the grey cement.
I bury him under his oak
he never reached
with all the acorns he could eat.

SHELL

Through a
crooked mouth

the sea
speaks to

me, a
sea creature

discarded from
home, a

brown freckled
rock; I

see blue
waves, white

sand, gulls,
lacquered gold.

APPLE TREE IN JUNE

A Christmas tree with green balls,
its leafy branches hang low,
bent with its burden of fruit.

Tart ripe apples
turn loose at a touch
or thump in the grass.

Smashed apples
rot on the ground,
the tree's summer surplus.

Cardinals and jays fly in and out,
sing, swing and feed,
gorge on the free feast.

Neighbors and friends fill baskets, bags,
make apple pies, apple sauce, apple crisp.
"The best I ever ate," they say.

SIX HAIKU

A robin, head cocked,
motionless, in grass, listens
for a worm to pass.

Hydrangea blossoms
beside my door, steal color
from the sky once more.

Shadowed, far below
the golden daffodil row,
violet faces show.

Yesterday's rosebud,
full-blown today, I cut
from the bush, throw away.

In the rotting cup
of the old oak stump, this spring
a peach tree came up.

With first morning light,
again songs of birds, silenced
by the dark last night.

PEACE AT CHRISTMAS

Closing the door,
I left the Christmas tree,
glittering lights,
metallic shine of tinsel,
boxes, gold and silver wrapped,
with red bows tied,
the jangle of Jingle Bells.

Deep in the garden
I looked at grey rain clouds,
black branches of winter trees.
Nothing glittered or glowed.
Only the red of berries,
the blue flash of bird's wing
colored the somber tones of peace.

RICHES OF NAPLES

"Some tourists remember the poverty of Naples," Mario said.
Dark children in gay-colored rags
At play in narrow dirty streets,
Lines of clothes strung from house to house,
Drying in dark canyons,
A one-legged beggar at the funiculare,
Holding out his tin cup, giving a smile for lire.
But every Neapolitan knows he is rich.

From the top of a hill in Castellemare
We looked down on the bay, at the blue water,
Held by the land in loving embrace.
We saw the twin peaks of Vesuvius,
Their heads in white clouds, guarding the distant shore.
Mario drew in his breath, stood tall with pride;
He caught my hand and smiled at the sea.
"These are the riches of Naples," he said.

GOD'S EYE

If God's eye is on the sparrow
why doesn't He see the cats,
lean, hungry, homeless,
meowing to me from the yard
and back porch steps?

As no manna falls from Heaven,
I put the bowl of milk
and plate of cold meat
beside the propped screen door
and wait inside.

They always come in quietly,
cautiously, sensing danger,
before they eat and drink.
Satisfied, they wash their faces,
and gaze at me through the glassed kitchen door.

Do they think I am God?

SHEDDING

As the oak tree, clothed in greenery
in summer, rounded, full,
protected from the sun,
in autumn sheds its leaves,
exposes bare, lean branches,
shows a different form,
opens itself to winter's wind and snow.

So, I, learning to write,
shed my armored covering,
pride, insincerity, hypocrisy,
my protection from hurt,
my shell against communion,
and expose myself, show to the world
my true form, the inner me.

TO THE EQUESTRIAN STATUE OF ATATURK
IN IZMIR, TURKEY

High in the air, astride your marble horse,
you sit, Ataturk,
your cold eyes gazing out upon the Aegean.

If you could see the water,
blue and calm now,
no longer red with the blood of Greeks,

And Ankara, the city you planted in dry Anatolian dust,
and miles of paved roads filled with fast-moving cars
instead of plodding camels,

You would be proud of the country you fathered.
You would open your carved stone lips
and say, "Choc Guze!"—"Well done."

ELM TREE

Like the death of
a friend

loss of the
elm tree

felled by the
sleet storm

in the main street
church yard.

HOME FROM THE HOSPITAL

Mamma, never ill herself,
who always nursed others,
rode from the car in a wheelchair
through fallen brown leaves
to her own front door.

She rested in bed,
watched the squirrels through her window,
smelled the vegetable soup
I cooked for supper.
"I'm home again," she said.

The next morning, hung to my arm,
she walked to the table for breakfast.
When I brought in the coffee,
she was sprawled on the floor,
red robe spread around her.
"Oh, Mamma, did you fall?" I said.
"Yes." Her last words: "I fell."

STRANGE CAT

The day I found him
crouched beside the kitchen door,
full-grown, hungry, dirty white,
he begged to come in.

I asked no questions
about his background,
his disposition.
I opened my door, accepted him.

Only love I gave him
and food and warm shelter,
even shared my bed,
until the night

He bit me fiercely,
sank four teeth into my thumb
as I stroked his furry head
close beside my pillow.

I locked him from my room,
sobbed with the pain
that shot all the way
up my arm to my heart.

Little I know of cat maleness
and hormones pounding in the blood.
Was this bite a strange act
of animal affection?

Or a thrust from the past,
his answer to a former
master's blow, or his defense
against a jungle ancestor?

Now I well know
whoever gives love should
prepare himself for pain.
Let him live, I say.

MARY BELLE CAMPBELL

Mary Belle Campbell of Whispering Pines, world traveler and free-lance writer, turned poet in 1974. Ms. Campbell was accepted by the North Carolina Poetry Society and won three Honorable Mentions in her first year.

She published *Moore County Sandhills USA, A North Carolina Celebration*, for a multi-media gallery show at the Southern Pines Library in June 1978.

Her poems, both traditional and terse free verse, have appeared in several literary magazines.

Since neither a trip to China (1978) nor a month of study and writing at Ezra Pound's castle retreat in Italy (1977) seems too far to travel, Ms. Campbell thinks nothing of frequently driving to Raleigh, Chapel Hill, or Carrboro, to Asheville, Laurinburg, or Charleston to read or to attend a workshop.

ITALIAN SUMMER

WAKING AT SCHLOSS BRUNNENBURG

"I want to come back to Brunnenburg to die." — Ezra Pound, in a letter to his daughter, Princess Mary de Rachewiltz, Discretions.

> Bird song   flute song
> full-throated solo
> above
>   morning's
>   obligato
> ringing clear
> from lone sequoia
> new world
>   memories
> transplanted.
>
> A song winging up
> to my Roman tower
> from the castle fort's
> crenellated terrace.

Bird song
ringing clear
exuberant   sure
ecstatic
          Pentecostal
glossolalia
spirit filled
a voice
I could understand.

Unlike the disembodied
dirge
of valley bells ring-
ing   rising sheer
from village steeples
burdening steep inclined
vineyards
valley walls.

Valley bells
tolling   toll-
ing   knells
faintly
they echo
echo
        di-
          min-
              u-
                en-
                  do.

Brunnenburg
Tirolo di Merano, Italia
Pentecost 1977

WIND FROM THE ALPS

"the ingle of Circe. . .in the timeless air"—E. P., Canto XXXIX

       Circe screams
       lost spirits rise
       fall
       voices drop-
       ing   dropping
       down   to
       San Pietro's bone house
       below the cliff.

       Windows rattle
       doors slam
       shutters fall
       glass shatters
       clatters to terrace below.

       Lightning flares
       wind whistles whines howls
       round   and round
       Brunnenburg's   Roman
       watch tower.

       Hail sweeps horizontal
       up the chasm
       like dust
       from an angry broom.

                      Brunnenburg Castle
                      Dorf Tirol, Italy

CLIFF SWALLOWS IN THE VAL DI TIROLO

In silent duos   trios   quatros
from Merano on the plain below
flashing black and white
in a great flock   come the swallows
a feathered vortex   swirling.

In colors of Pagliacci
clowns   mimes
in rising gyre
up our narrow valley they fly.

Rondine   rondone   round and round
above green yellow treetops
acacias   acacias in bloom
veering   gliding
skimming the cliffs

On and on   the harlequins come
drop-
     ing
        glis-
            san-
                do
a unison of   somatic voices soaring
ever
    high-
        er
          and
             higher
expanding in volume
a mathematician's pencilled
cylinder
    rhythm
        ellipsed.

Vivaldi's music
          heard
      inside
   the

middle ear
til above our castle's highest
          crenellated
tower
into the cliff's refuge
                    one
          by
      one
    they
disappear.

Dorf Tirol
Brunnenburg 1977

THE SEER
A Lifetime Glimpsed

"we who have passed over Lethe" —*E. P., Canto LXXIV*

      An able mind   ages old
      curiosity
      unquenchable thirst
         to know truth
      hunger
         to experience   to love
      a vision of Paradise
      an obsession
         to translate   transmit
      his story of civilization
      Kulchur
      and courage
         to speak
         to cleave
      like Agamemnon
         at Aulis.

                                    Ezra Pound's Library
                                    Brunnenburg Castle

THE GIFT

"the light there almost solid"—E. P., Canto XCIII

From a long tradition
of fired sand, silica and ash
    Pompeii's volcanic obsidian
    Rome's blown bottles for
        Pompeia's perfume
    Venetian millefiore glass
        twisted into
        candelabra and
        chandeliers
        for the haute
        bourgeoisie
comes my morning glass of water
resting on an apartment-size
        Frigidaire.

From long reach of sun's fiery corona
through double columned window
comes light from Dolomite dawn
on clean Alpine air.

In this Roman towered
age accumulated castle
breakfast and books
        scattered on
        blue painted
        peasant table with its
        hearts and flowers
begin my day.

Over my shoulder this bright
Italian ray strikes
my half-filled jelly glass
        Tyrolean spring water
        sand filtered
        high underground
        an Alpen stream.

Suddenly motorized by its
interior need to cool
the miniature Frigidaire
begins to vibrate, to create
an optic phenomenon.

A spectral universe
prismatic water
fracturing the rays, as a diamond
        a rainbow of splendour.
A gem-like shimmer encompasses
the little water glass.
Crystal, not from Merano.

Patrizia's Apartment
Schloss Brunnenburg

PILGRIMAGE

"the rose in the steel dust. . ."—E. P., Canto LXXIV

We tramp Piazza San Marco
search for flower sellers
we walk to Riva degli Schiavoni
seeking flower market stalls
finally board the vaporetto
for San Michele   funeral island.

We find magnolia   blooming
beyond the cloister garden
pass by stacked up Venetian families
racked up   in marble files.

Behind the arch in unkempt
Auslanders Cemetery
we find your stone   circle of ivy
courage red begonia.

We are guests   arrived
without a gift, Ezra.
Your three roses
we plucked from a bush
bravely blooming
before another's tomb.

11 June 1977
Venice, Italy

TIDES MOVING

Venice
early   early morning
gangs of youth
couples of 12 and 15 years
children still
knapsacked   backpacked
chute out
from the maze
of streets
            of hostels
            cheap hotels.

They wash across
Piazza San Rocco
to vaporetto stop
Stelle San Toma
an undisciplined flood.

Human
      plastic
      flotsam
floats away
on the tide.

Canal Grande
            absorbs
            all
even its mossy places
mist breaking
shimmer of sun surging in
on the tide.

                    Scuola San Rocco
                    Venezia

VENEZIA REVISITED – AVE ATQUE VALE

Today we depart Serenissima
most exalted of cities
Canal Grande in mourning
mist and fog   fog over water
snatches away my breath
fades Oriental palaces
to Monet canvasses   at dawn
Rouen cathedrals in half light.

Listen!   In the void
the vaporetto   a mauve-gray
wraith   cuts the swish   wash
motoscapo motors rush   pass hush.
Nauseating sweetness   from
honey-suckled wall   smells
of fetid dampness   sweep by.

I sense the dying   the undying beauty
restored churches   murals peeling
mouldy museums canvasses cracking
fading scaling plaster palazzios
paint over putrefaction
lacquer over powdering mosaic
sub-divided flats   in neglected palaces
first floors abandoned   empty
rotting in rain.   Watery catacomb.

Venice
12 June 1977

VENI, VIDI, VICIT
I CAME, I SAW, IT CONQUERED ME

Venice
flushed us out
by fast diesel
to shores of Lago di Garda
Lake Garda   bluest of lakes.

A taxi drove us
straight from the station
across the draw
through Sirmione's
fourteenth century walls.

No arrows fell
from castle
fortifications
no cries rose
from donjon keep.

No donkeys, no pushcarts
only pedestrians
crowding old town lanes
an arms' spread wide.

Oleander and palm up-turn
worn cobbles. No cars
only our taxis wind these
tourist-filled streets.

Yellowed stone houses
now boutiques   flaunt
second-story red geranium
window boxes — new banners
for new conquerors
an old tradition.

In Sirmione, it is said
all men become poets
even warriors' sons

witness, Verona-born
off-to-Rome Catullus.

His father's troops   horse-weary
Roman soldiers   discovered
thermal springs   off-shore
(before Christ sampled
Roman might   and   justice).

Here on high promontory
Sirmione's narrow breast
Catullus the General built
his brick villa   stylish baths
extant to this day crumbling
stone corridors   conduits.
One remaining arch
two columns twelve meters high
make the only mystery.

Below the Tyrolean Alps
this miniscule peninsula
"all-but-island"
Catullus said
full of stucco houses
and hotels today.

Ever a refuge
        fortified by Romans
        invaded by barbarian
        Lombards   Teutons
        Franks   The Church
        routed by Mussolini
        Fascists   hobnailed
        German soldiers
now over-run by German
and English tourists
Sirmione   still
teeming   today.

The taxi crawls
through crowds then

sweeps us past
sub-tropic
gardens, deposits us at our
sign-proclaimed "Bad Hotel"
(Bath Hotel).

Like horde-weary Romans
we bathe away our twentieth
century aches
in mineral baths, the hot waters
still gushing
from under
snowy hills
lipping
cobalt blue Lago di Garda.

Sirmione, Lake Garda
Lombardy, Italy, 1975, 1977

AN ELEGY FOR EZRA POUND
—for Olga Rudge and Mary de Rachewiltz

Ezra Pound, you dead?
You, who tried to write "Paradise?"

No, not while students and poets
Make pilgrimage across continents
    to Hailey, Idaho
    to the Beineke Library in New Haven
    to Philadelphia
    Rapallo, Roma
    Schloss Brunnenburg in Dorf Tirol
    to Trattoria Montin in Venezia
    and sit on the steps of the Doganna.

Not as long as anthologists include
    Robert Frost, W. C. W., Olson
    MacLeish, Joyce
    Amy, H. D., Marianne
    Old Possum's "Wasteland"
    Auden, Yeats, Bunting.

I crowd onto the vaporetto
Cross to San Michele — Funeral Island.
I stand beside your grave.
Bells toll. Overtones echo
    Mozart, Vivaldi.

I feel the press, the energies
Of a multitude of masks beside me
    cloaks
    Van Dykes
    blue jeans
    multiple Personae
Heads bowed in silent
Gratitude.

                              Venezia
                              11 June 1977

SIRMIONE GLIMPSED THROUGH MIST

"O silvery Sirmio,"—Tennyson

Glimpsed through mist and gentle rain
On blue Lake Garda's faded shore
A ghostly Roman villa — old Sirmione's
Gigantic crumbling arches, toppled columns.

In mist and gentle rain
I walk these ruins again
Consul, censor, senator
Haunting old Sirmio's gathering place.
Did Caesar in Verona visit here?

Fallen bricks shout Caesar's power
Rain-shrouded broken conduits
Once thermal baths loudly protest
Young Catullus' leisure
His poetic cult removed to raucous Rome.

I wander trance-like
In these millennial groves among
Scarred emaciated
Still silvery-green twisting
Olive-bearing olive trees.

Centuries' ancient wraiths
Watch me
Cry out to me.

Sirmione, Lago di Garda
Lombardia, Italia
August 1975

TIROLO DI MERANO

*"the most splendid view over two open valleys. . .
endless ranges of mountains"* —Mary de Rachewiltz, Discretions

Today in Autumn
prophetic ivy
is flaming the walls
yellow-red
above green-black firs
soon to be blanched
blanketed   in snow.

When first I came
to this village
its battlemented terrace
seemed a balcony
to the world —
terrazzo del mundo.
Chestnuts — castagnas —
bloomed pale pink
perfuming the valley.

Today and tomorrow
mahogany chestnuts
repeat their round
burst their burrs
plummet to earth
joining this contested terra
in one more "farewell."

*Rimmele Terrace
Dorf Tirol, 1977*

THE FLORENTINE CRAFTSMAN
A Retrospective View in Heroic Couplets

"He wrapped them up in expensive green silk."
—C. F. Cavafy, tr. by Edmund Keeley

At dusk the goldsmith lovingly withdrew
His masterpiece, a charm, from window view
A lovely bauble, eighteen amethyst lights
Inlaid in handcrafted gold lantern sights.

He wrapped it reverently in jeweler's cloth
I sensed he treasured it and to sell was loath.
I bargain, I visit the jeweler three days
Admire the cendalos — the charms — that he displays.

One charm, a coral-mounted gold pagoda
Its roofs, tier on tier, with shimmering aura.
Another, Midas-rich, gold, polished
A Turkish lamp, with topaz crown embellished.

And still, no amethyst-inlaid lantern
Until, growing friendly, he brings out an urn
A chalice, repousee in Christian symbols.
He presents it proudly, full of tiny thimbles

For fingers deft in Gobelin needle skills.
Beneath a gray silk cloth, he now unveils
Overcome with pride, confidence and caprice
With reckless dignity, his masterpiece

The cherished amethyst-mounted cendalo.
I cannot buy it. The craftsman cannot let it go.

Firenze, 1966

ADMONITIONS

Angry I
in Venice old
I refused to enter
the Doge's Palace   on
surging tide of tourists.
I saw St. Mark's under water
felt futility   at such beauty
carved stone   copper sculpture
mosaic pavement.

Years ago in museum galleries
I felt strange antipathies
for Venetian art.
My skin   bristled
with admonitions.

I still shiver at Tintoretto's
funnels of light.   Though I stood
in front of his home   I could not
enter—ghostly studio.
In Gardone d'Annunzio's decor
repulsed me.   I fled his house
mausoleum   of memories
forgotten memories.

Have I
unfinished lives?
reconciliations due?
that lead me
back   again   and again
to Italy?

Venezia, 1970, 1977

EUGENE V. GRACE

Eugene Grace is a practicing ophthalmologist in Durham, North Carolina, and a man of varied interests. A graduate of the University of Michigan Medical School, he came to North Carolina as a general physician and later specialized at the University of North Carolina. He has been or is a director of numerous organizations and is active in Lionism. He maintains high levels of interest in government, education, and literature as well as medicine. His travels include professional work in third world nations, and he draws upon all this experience for his poetry. He is married and the father of four children.

OUR SILVER SILENCE

A silver silence filled our kingdom
When a strange piping sound we heard.
Hearing, we followed hand in hand,
Walking among lowland flowers,
Seeing the filling tide of light,
Smelling fragrance of meadow-sweet,
Tasting the sweetness of morning dew,
Feeling the closeness of each other,
Knowing we were in our place,
That we'd awaken from this dream
And struggle for its remembrance
And settle for a dimmer sense
Of the clear beauty that filled it.

A POEM FOR OTHERS

This poem is not for you;
Yours it could never be.
It's for those others who
Cannot love, nor be free.

For those who follow injury,
Who walk grassless paths,
Who shout about the day
And beat against flowing hope.

Who watch the rising sun
And wonder when the rain.
Who coldly watch twilight
And fear what it will bring.

Who dream drastic dreams
And hold in ridicule, love.
Who with selfish holdings
Proclaim the profane.

Who live in shadowed life
And cannot now emerge,
Yet cannot shadows endure
When darkness fills the heart.

This poem is not for you;
Yours it could never be.
It's for those others who
Cannot love, nor be free.

FOR CAROL, LYDIA, AND OTHER DOLLYS

Well, hello, Dolly, where've you been?
Have I been just passing you by,
Seeing you as other women,
Not knowing what you mean to me?

Dolly, a long time I've known you
But your eyes never seemed so bright;
Never more seemed your wit and charm
And your beauty becomes twilight.

You have now returned love to me,
Bringing bright music to my mind,
Setting my heart singing anew,
Seeking all the love it can find.

Oh, Dolly, this is our summer
Passing gently into autumn,
Finding something to remember
Of our own to hold forever.

LEONARDO'S ELIZABETTA

In Paris where first I met her,
Midst soft lights and shadows,
Before mountains rising to sky,
She wore velvet and satin
And smiled me a woman's smile
That filled my mind with lyrics.
He must have loved her, too,
In other ways I cannot know
Or cannot truly understand
In even five centuries more.
For a thousand days he saw her
And teamed with loss to create
The smile she smiles to me
From out her sad, tender beauty.
By any other name, the same,
Leonardo's, my Elizabetta.

I'LL CATCH HER A SEASON

If only I could catch the seasons
How happy I would be.
First I'd catch Spring and Fall
And hold for you to see.

Winter I'd grab with mittened hands
And quickly throw from me,
Beyond Spring, then bring back Fall
And hold for you to see.

Summer I'd let bide awhile
While you were close to me;
Then I'd cool its scorching heat
With Spring for you to see.

I'll try to find a season handle
Or borrow a net from the sea;
Then surely catch Spring and Fall
And hold for you to see.

If no handle or net I find,
No season edge or tail I see,
Nothing to catch and hold to,
I'll hold you, leave seasons free.

SHE'S COMING HOME

A full moon it was when we met
And a full moon has brought you back.
I had searched for your eyes in others
That never were so clearly deep and lovely
And I'd looked for natural smiles like yours
But had found them not with you gone from me.

No longer happy strangers that we knew,
Trees then wept their loneliness, cried for you;
Spring seemed somehow by a strange force delayed,
As though bad timing or connection made,
As though on hold for some coming event,
As though she wondered where little girls went.

Upon the warm and greening earth I fell
And pressed my ear tightly against the ground
And thought I heard your footsteps, tiptoeing
In dancing shoes, softly through reason's door.
Again I pressed, every earth sound to hear
And heard Spring whispering, she's coming home.

INTRUSION

She moved against me
In sleep.
Her body was warm and soft.
Softly murmured were
Her sighs.

I opened my eyes
To night.
My happiness welled, then stilled.
Then, she moved again,
Again.

She was loving you
That night,
Calling you in murmured sighs
From out the shadows,
From dreams.

The stars were cold bright,
And clear.
Finally sleep etched the night,
And this intruder
Was gone.

She'll not say your name,
Ever.
I'll not ask about that night
Which is yours and hers,
Ever.

COALESCENCE

I have turned from you,
Left you standing alone
Many times, in many places.
I'd never have you be
Merely a lovely catalogue
Of those things I see;
Nor would I want you
To ever only cerebral be;
For I'd never, never
Presume to caress you
With heavy hands of logic.
I'd rather leave you again,
Alone, on pages of my mind,
Waiting for coalescence
To make a poem of you.

MEMORIES COMPANIONS MAKE

Memory comes quietly,
Walking on tiptoes,
Slipping into thoughts.
Coming in soft shadows,
Fleshing out in evenings,
Comforting aloneness,
Memory comes quietly.
Could I but keep her
Locked within my room,
Away from the silent night
And the cold, dark street,
And run her rosary
Of long forgotten thoughts,
Would I less lonely be?

SECOND MOVEMENT

I hear a rhapsody of sadness
And must find in it some joy.
Someday she'll go from me
And I shall know not when.
It may have already been,
The tender music of a sad song,
Like light flashing from a distant star
And streaking for a million years
And breaking now before my eyes,
Composed, played, now to realize.

She cannot know its strains,
Only that they play on her heart.
Time tossed in a world strange to her,
She feels need for new tides,
An elsewhere search for self
That she must make beyond me,
Beyond time and place that I know,
Beyond the shores of present love.
I must hear her song of sadness
And find the few notes of gladness.

WILL SOMEONE LOOK

Milton sang his fine, translunar music
Long before I knew keenness that was his,
Shakespeare's clear, boundless humanity
Will live throughout eternity,
Shelley's words reached dazzling heights
That I can never hope to reach,
Coleridge knew the magic end of day
That spins mystery into twilight,
And Byron found passion in anger
As well as in his soulful joy.
When I come to lay me down
Beside my words true and clear
Will someone look at them and say
He wrote of love and life, and loved.

AN ODE TO LOVE

Daughter of Love,
Mother, Mistress too,
Across the years
Haunts your beauty.

Never one of shadows,
You lead from shadows
Along far-flung paths
Among visions of light.

Your mystic shape
And star-lit brightness,
Unchanged by time's tempest,
Rolls heaven before me
When you touch my hand.

Sought by kings are you;
Even my princely heart
That breaks to tear for you,
Seeks to see your brighter eye.

A MYSTIC MOUNTAIN

My mind is a mystic mountain
That lets you in, then slams the door;
Yet opens time and time again
For beauty seen, to love the more.

Love must have returned you to me;
A hundred years is ne'er too soon.
Since you have bid my mind be free
You are my maid of Brigadoon.

I see you on my mountain ridge,
Against the wispy, misty sky,
Dimly, across our hidden bridge
Where love and you first met my eye.

No Weser washes my town wall
Nigh wondrous portal opened wide.
I've lived in Hamelin not a'tall;
Yet you, bright music dwell inside.

My mind is a mystic mountain
That lets you in, then slams the door;
Yet opens time and time again
For beauty seen, to love the more.

ON VISITING JOHN KEATS

When I looked for your tomb
During a cold, drizzly rain,
(One that you'd have avoided)
I found you not in place
And now must correct my guide.

Today I came rightly by
And left roses there for you,
Thinking you'd have liked that.
Others will do that, too, John,
For a thousand years or more,
Will hear your words echoing
As long as they know romance.

Perhaps you read my thoughts,
(Surely no need to speak them
To one who dwells elsewhere)
But suppose that you were there,
I had voiced and you had heard
Better you would understand
That every land hears your words,
That the ground in which Keats lies
By Roman guides should be known,
No less than with Marcellus
By theater fame now known
And high-mourned by Virgil's poem;
As did he, you died too soon.

IN TIMES OF WONDER

No quest for roots this; no quest at all.
It's just good to be back here again,
By the ocean sunlit after the rain.
Beauty is as beauty was, unfading
And unchanging in its withdrawing roar.
Unchanging too are the cradling hills,
Palm-lined and stately in their palisades.
Remember now before memory fades
And keep your mind wide and mystic and free.

A little teahouse stands where once she lived.
Is there now a trace of change on her face?
Across the crowded years haunts her beauty,
For love is beauty now to remember.
I walked alone today where once we walked,
The sun-warmed sand beneath our rapturous feet,
Remembering happy laughter in her voice
That easily came always as we talked.
Not other would I do if I had choice.

From the pier I watched our sun disappear.
Wind blown are many dreams that once we had.
We faced the sun and left shadows behind,
Like moments just before the sudden dawn,
Finding the bright beauty our hearts must know.
Tossed and blown were our dreams while they did last.
Sometimes I hear a quiet voice whisper
And I almost forget that she's not mine.

What once we had now should be gone away;
Sunday is along the way to Monday.
When she once lived in my unconsciousness
Then she didn't upset my mind at all.
Lately my mind seeks to find our moments,
Precious few to recall our happiness
That didn't last this quarter century past.
Yet she still tiptoes in my silent mind
And returns to me in times of wonder.

LEON HINTON

Leon Carrington Hinton was born in October 1926 in Danville, Virginia, but has lived in the Burlington, North Carolina, area most of his life. He started to write actively about five years ago when he joined the Burlington Writer's Club. He will be the president of the club for the 1979-80 year and is on the board of directors of the North Carolina Poetry Society.

Writing short stories is his first love, but because of limited time to devote to writing, he started writing poetry. He has won awards on a local and state level for his prose and poetry and has had feature stories published in local newspapers.

Mr. Hinton makes his living in the computer and accounting areas and moonlights at a local technical institute teaching subjects related to these two fields.

GOODBYE

Meeting you was like
opening a window
in a musty room,
long closed.

The fresh air rushed in
cleaning out corners
that didn't know
they needed it.

You say you'll return.
We know better.
There, you'll be
a catalyst, like here,

serving your new friends
as mentor, poet, lover;
lifting the place a tad,
making it yours.

ROSE, PRESSED IN WAX PAPER

I am young again remembering
that summer when we
like bionics, walked on water
leaped over tall buildings

touched the sky—
hung by our hands from
a sliver of moon
toes and lips touching

loved under the trees
hearts beating as one
you flew without wings out a window
all I have left is this rose.

SOAPBOX

you brought me up, Elizabeth
lived in our home
cooked and cleaned
for seven a week plus room and board
and still dressed better than mom
how did you smile at six a.m.
and cook a hearty meal
clean house and have supper ready
when we came home from school and work
wash and iron for a house full
and still remain cheerful
you never complained
thank you for giving me certain values
because of you
I've never known prejudice
only felt blessed to know you
and love you
so climb on that soapbox
and demand what's due you and yours
the world needs your recipe
for living

TICK FEVER

We found a tick on my arm.
Off it fell on me or her or
in the black floor carpet
of the car.
It's still at large.

Until we find a tick
in that car
or on one of us
we'll live with it
sleep with it

feel it crawl slowly
through our scalps
in our ears
across our bodies
everywhere, yes EVERYWHERE

and have visions
of our friends
and loved ones
weeping over our coffins saying
"and it was just a little tick."

NO MORE DRAGGING MAIN

When I look up my beloved Main Street
and behold the havoc Urban Renewal
has wrought, I cringe.

Mall they call it—
looks more like a tornado struck
leaving multi-level roofs
falling over each other,
with plants springing up
in unlikely places.

Walking through this mall
you dare not look in store windows.
You must watch where you walk
or you lunge into space
over an unexpected wall.

No nostalgia here—only improvement.
Taxpayer's burden, robbing me of sights
that brought memories of dragging Main
on a Saturday night in hot pursuit
of romance in a parked car.

IRON WILL

I will not smoke this cigarette
that smells so good.
I can't. I have no match.
This time I know I have
the power to give them up.

They stain my teeth
smell up my clothes
and foul my breath
and goodness knows
may cause my death.

I quit!
I know I can!
I will not smoke this cigarette
that smells so good!
Pardon me, do you have a light?

LAMENT

Beautiful girl
Glancing around
Expecting someone.

I want to tell you about life,
            love, pitfalls.
I want to be your surrogate father,
Your confidant.

Here he comes.
Looking like your father.
He is your lover.
I am sad.

SKI KING

How do I ski?
Sideways, backwards
horizontally.

How do I ski?
Unorthodoxically.

CLICHE PARENTS

puritan couple
tough as nails
salt of the earth
good as gold
busy as bees
generous to a fault
(even to strangers)
always there
when you need them

RECURRENCE

in the night
when all is magnified
the hurt, the unjustness of it
comes over, inundating
like waves rolling over a beach
again. . .again. . .again. . .again
each wave a distinct separate thing
yet all part of the whole
the ocean, the big hurt
until finally, the tide recedes
from the shores of the mind
and peace comes
and sleep comes

WHOOP TE DO

pretty girls
with well coiffed hair
and stylish clothes
of them 'tis said
they are less apt
to be good in bed

but take one
with a plump rump
who's not so neat
but really sweet
like one I knew
and WHOOP TE DO

STARBURST

I saw her today,
dignified, poised, every
hair in place   nothing
like the wild one I
was with that night

the stars rained
down   gathered in a spinning
ball   gained momentum
                more than sound
            before EXPLODING
        skyward
to resume their places

save one that stayed
a problem to be dealt with

she shows no sign
that she remembers
but that was
light years ago

TRIP

she cared
that snow-sniffing beauty
cared so much
when he left
she went on a bird flight
into oblivion
using a different snow

when she landed
she didn't know
where she'd been
how long she'd stayed
the jaundiced liver and
fluidless prune-like
body healed

but not the mind
still in a fog
she spends her time
trying to recall
how it was
and who he was
when she cared

LOIS HOLT

Lois Holt, a native of Durham, North Carolina, began writing during high school and had her first poems published in *An Anthology of High School Poetry*. During the fourteen-year period she lived in Raleigh, she was a regular contributor to "Today's N.C. Poem," which appeared in *The News and Observer* and was the subject of a feature article for this column. Her poems also have appeared in *The Raleigh Times*. At that time, she was a member of the Longview Writers.

Mrs. Holt is currently chairman of the Friday Noon Poets, a gathering of Piedmont poets who meet weekly in Carrboro, North Carolina. As chairman she worked with the staff of the Morehead Planetarium to produce the original presentation of "Poetry Under the Stars" and has served as editorial chairman for the ensuing anthology. She is a member of the North Carolina Poetry Society and has recently been asked to assume editorial chairmanship for the society's pending anthology.

She is employed by an insurance company in Chapel Hill, North Carolina, and resides in Durham with her husband and two teen-age sons.

KNOWING

I knew, before knowing, that it wouldn't be enough
to recite "Annabel Lee" (because you ask), compare
rhythm and rhyme, the intrusion—inclusion—of
gods and goddesses, speaking of abstract things,
Byron and Keats, "The Rhyme of the Ancient Mariner."

I knew, before knowing, that it wouldn't be enough
to taste the same wine, smell the same smoke,
break crackers with cheese, hold lemon cookies
in my mouth until they melted, cupping cups in
hands that trembled from want of touching.

Knowing that you knew.

TO ONE WHO WILL KNOW

She found her bargains in the basement,
Remnants, seconds, irregulars;
Pausing in her pursuit
Of "A PENNY SAVED — A PENNY EARNED,"
Long enough to let the softness of voile
Draping the first-floor mannequin
Slip through her fingers.
She took for herself the back of the chicken,
Saying it was her favorite;
Stripping the cavities of its two morsels,
And drawing on the bone for any flavor of meat
                that remained.
I spoke of steak. . .
She offered brown crumbs to bribe me into silence,
Knowing that I would take for myself
The breast of the chicken.

PA'S HOME

Pa's home!
Run to the field,
Hide in the barn,
Crawl in the corncrib
And pull the baby in;
Wiggle under the wagon,
Cower in the corner,
Cling to the petticoat of
One raped in drunken rage;
Cover your ears from the crying
And damn the man.

BUT NAMES

Say the name!

It slithers along the vocal cords
coiled for the kill
scorching the tip of a tongue
coated in venom.

But I am immune to the bite
having suffered the tortures
of innoculation.

OVER COCKTAILS (WITH RHETT BUTLER)

Had we met?
He thought he knew — had known
the same green eyes,
hair pushed up, piled high.
Slipping a strap,
peeling the crepe,
consuming the flesh, seen and unseen,
with a gaze that penetrated even to Scarlet.

SECOND THOUGHTS

We've talked of this before. . .
The superiority of our intelligence,
Belittling by disregarding.
She had said, "The coming of the Lord
            draws nigh."

Hogwash!

But now, looking to the mountain,
I contemplate the security of its caverns.

ASHES TO ASHES
DUST TO DUST

On still nights,
When heat lightning hints of rain,
And talk turns to tobacco,
I think of Pa
Bellowing like a pregnant heifer,
Lathered like his plowin' mule;
Cussin' the carriage that separated
His ashes to ashes from mine.
He went, like snuffing the wick,
Never to know that I came back
To sit in sight of his stone,
And damn my days
From dust to dust.

IN TRUST

Take him...
But remember
That he belongs to me.
There are no strings to cut,
He was severed from the cord
To remain as the fawn to the doe by choice;
He will be to you one of the flock,
Obeying according to the pitch of your voice;
Responding to me, "Because."
I cannot anticipate the comparisons,
The idolatries;
But, today, he is weaned.
I will not stand at the door
To wave, and wave, and wave,
But will kiss him goodbye
(A natural thing with us),
Turn to my tasks,
And weep.

THE CHRISTMAS CREPE

She called it her Christmas crepe,
Leaving it to hang from eve to eve
Segregated from the crush of a too-small closet.
Removing the muslin (a second) and lifting the
Scented, white satin hanger from the hook
On the back of the bedroom door;
Holding the crepe at arm's length ("It'll do.")
Aired and pressed for the pouring of punch
(a $3.98 bowl and cups); reversing the ritual,
Leaving it to hang from eve to eve.

A GIFT

I'll give you a rose,
Yellow — my favorite.
Not white — for virtue was lost
When the candles were capped,
Not red — for the promise of a pagan
Princess to puff your pillow;
But yellow — a compromise.

BEQUEATH

The watch?
Yes, very old;
It belonged to one who pushed the plow,
My father and his.
Held by the chain
To swing back and forth between their knees,
Marking the births and deaths of three generations.
It runs still, you see,
Always accurate,
Having been wound at exactly nine o'clock every night;
A habit I mimic.

REFLECTIONS

It's been years. . .
But I know the place,
Having picked blackberries there
In the summer of my ninth year;
Balanced on the splitrail like a Ringling acrobat,
The song of the swing is with me still.
We were from the city,
An affliction cured with well water and cornbread;
You say the house is gone,
A pity.

TESTING

You dictated —
Denoting the distance and direction
Of devotion's daring;
You lectured —
And I listened; listing the limitations
Of love's longings.
You read the rules —
Pausing between the Dos and Don'ts,
Shoulds and Shouldn'ts,
Woulds and Wouldn'ts,
Coulds and Couldn'ts
To council on the complications of commitment.
You queried —
And I ask if you graded on the curve.

AT THE POINT

Down at the point,
Passed the bottles, beer cans,
Beachbums and Harlow hussies,
Gulls wade;
Boats bob beyond the chips
Chewed and spit back like some whore,
Had and discarded;
Water's edge — walk the waves,
At the point,
Gulls wade.

LOVE POEM

If you must go
then read for me a love poem
no sad sonnets of sorrow
whisper of wanting
caressing with clear, hand-cut words
that crystalize and tinkle in my mind
like bells tolling, tolling for me.

ALEX HUTCHINS

James Alexander Hutchins III spent his childhood between Alexandria, Virginia, and Cairo, Egypt, where he later graduated from high school. A year at the American University in Cairo was followed by five years in the Navy, and for two years Mr. Hutchins travelled extensively throughout the United States and Europe. He holds a degree in English from Elon College in Elon College, North Carolina. In August 1979, Mr. Hutchins entered the Babcock Graduate School of Management at Wake Forest University to pursue an MBA degree.

A man of interests ranging from the medical field and microbiological studies to the humanities, Mr. Hutchins is a painter and a photographer. An in-depth knowledge of printing, layout, photography, and the graphic arts aided him in the publication of *Reflections in Thought*, a book of his poetry brought out in 1977. Mr. Hutchins became executive director of the Alamance County Arts Council in July 1977.

                    FEAR

            There
              is a
                blessed
                  agony
                    being
                  ashamed
                      of
                        the
                          fear
                          in
                            one's
                              self.

ENTANGLEMENTS

Kind and sensuous lips
announce their subtle intent
reminding me of
entanglements and love
never to be shared.

EYES

Beneath the dark hair her
eyes, soft and caring, naively
took away my fears,
held me
    and briefly
        I was hers.

CHANGES

We are shielded by the
loose fitting clothes of
our failures, and yet
we continually change our
dress to the seasons
of our dreams.

WINTER'S PASSING

The warmth of the new sun
penetrates the window and my
eyes put aside the cold
darkness of the long winter
and relax with the muskrat
as it swiftly and gently
glides across the pond
of my mind.

LITTLE MISS NO-NAME

And as her self-centered parents
ignored her precious needs,
the child withdrew to the corner
of her room and cowered there
with her favorite doll who
she addressed as Little Miss No-Name.

HEIGHTS OF UNHAPPINESS

Crew-cut mountains with your icy wind March deadness,
stand erect among those who have fallen.
Valley willow weeps from your breath.
Grey veils cloud your vision of times yet to be.
Moss lined paths hold the dew of your veins.
Asphalt threads scar your ancient body.
Early mourning tears cleanse the monuments of your weakness.
Pensive pine and spruce guard the mysteries
that were once yours alone.
Time's crippled currents are the pools you must bathe in
as thoughtless humans unravel your serenity.
Garbage piles of decadence are your children's final playground.

DEATH'S REJECTION

Out of the darkness she came and
fastened onto me like a leech,
purging me of the mockery
I had for mankind.
Her decayed skull echoed
with Hell's rejoicing triumph.
The void of her mouth, in
whispers, beckoned to be held.
The temptive calmness of her breath
evoked quivering sensations trembling
off my layers, blending with
apprehensive tears of my discomfort.
Tombstone eyes pierced my nakedness
drawing me into silhouetted arms.
Violent screams muted by the flow of
poisoned blood filled the cavities
of my lost security, as
She returned to the darkness.

A BURIAL OF AN UNKNOWN CHILD

Few witnessed the end of the day
as crowds spoke words of kindness.
Few understood the meaning of sound
when mourners heard cries of sorrow.
Women carried hearts in their hand;
Men wore their souls under heel.
Controlled feelings echoed words' passion
rented for the living, not dead.
Introverted smiles, repressed love, all
injected at birth with ancestral grace.
Robed thoughts comforting not, lay silent
on the ground enshrining Earth's child.

TWO TOGETHER

They stood facing each other
their bodies transfixed,
rigid,
silent,
like the Sphinx staring
at its reflection on the
surface of the Great Pyramid.

Slowly their arms rose
simultaneously passing
erect,
shoulders,
and with the force of a
butterfly's wind, rested in
front between them.

Their hands connected with
chalk fingers interlacing
one,
together,
while their bodies playfully
moved in Minuet fashion;
poised heads swayed in the air,
as their feet sailed around the
perimeters of the ice.

ROBERT JACKSON

In an Argentine high school, Mr. Jackson was introduced to poetry by the footnotes to T. S. Eliot's "Wasteland." Later, he courted his wife with the musical refrains of W. B. Yeats. He was deeply influenced by Whitman while in college, Pound in graduate school, and Dante in Italy. Currently, he is a member of the department of mathematics at Duke University.

DAPHNIS AND CHLOE

Have you seen summer's moist early morning mist
cleft by the sun's golden rays, then set so free?
Or forest green gloom transfused by one bright thrust?

Then have you seen her countenance shine on me,
she who is the calming down of the tempest;
say the sun and the moon, or the balming sea.

THE DICTIONARY'S DEFINITION OF 'DEEP'

That profound impression found
in a bottomless abyss
among the veils of mystery
around a woman's beauty.

WHOSE CHILDREN?

Were you to wait with a woman long enough
she would impregnate your sensibilities,
gazing out empty grey windows, ill at ease,
secretly she'd whisper, silencing beauty:
"Whose children are these, thus willed by me to thee?"

OUR GEOLOGY

Early in earth's long history
there was only one large land mass
engirdled by a global sea.
Then, the continents came to pass,
and drifted away from each other,
you on one; I upon another.

KYRIE ELEISON

Midst the dead of winter there revives that child
who resurrected by the Roman terror,
will wash away our well-intended error;
thence, render us again both tender and mild.

WATER LILIES

Events that flow
through our fingers,
that we allow
to pass us by.

I CHING

Mountains standing close together
the image wet, yet keeping still
beyond thy thought, un-wandering.

A crane calling in the shade,
its young answering lowly
near these goblets
that were mine, but now are thine.

THE ITALIAN GIGOLO

The pictures I draw of the people I know
tell me this society is aristocratic.
Awkwardly, I admit that it is not mine,
nor can I think their fashionable thoughts.
Having been stripped of this, my last illusion,
they shall not take from me my beggar priest.

CORPORATE SOULS

Damn their corporate souls in whose name
they perpetuate inhumanity and injustice,
absent-mindedly ignoring all men the same.

OUR BODY POLITIC

Were you and I to be born
children of some other era
when meat were staff of life,
we would have been butchers.

THE FIRST STAGE

I heard on the radio that
"most women do not reach orgasm
during normal intercourse and that
clitoris fore-play is essential for that."

But touching them anywhere
preludes even that maneuver,
and the gentlest touch of all
is done by one mind imprinting
its patterns upon another.

Later, the radio said that
"the objective of the first stage
was to leave the woman
in an after-glow of happiness:
Try to insure that they remain
content in all the things that they
must do, from day to day, today;
until you can return to them."

THE SECOND STAGE

The sexual act is completed
by the delivery of the new-born babe.
I know only one class of men
who do this for its pure, simple beauty.

They are now called obstetricians;
they go around assisting the women
of other men who must still miss
the wonder and plain truth of this event.

MITCHELL FORREST LYMAN

Mitchell Forrest Lyman was born on April 1, 1918 in northern Virginia near Farmers Fork. She has lived in Virginia, Florida, Maryland, and California. Mrs. Lyman came to North Carolina in 1968. For six years she has coordinated a poetry workshop, the Poetry Cooperative, which meets in the Reserach Triangle area. A poet by compulsion, Mrs. Lyman is a member of the North Carolina Poetry Society and has had her poems published in *The Crucible, The Sun,* and *The Chapel Hill Newspaper.*

SHADES OF MEANING

Truth comes clothed in varied garbs;
Hand-me-downs are what rumors wear;

Falsehood shades its eyes with many masks,
While candor's coat is always clear.

Now when I go out along the streets,
It's rainbow colors I parade in;

But when I meet a friend of true insight,
It's Eve's Undress that I'm arrayed in!

STUB OF A PENCIL

When failing to reverse the earth,
One's impotence produces rage,
There's a therapeutic worth
In scribbling on the page.

TO A TRAVELING HUSBAND

Here on the pillow the musk
    of you clings;
When will the all
    of you return?

I hold this remnant,
    and wait
To be wrapped again
    in the whole cloth.

THE NEXT STEP

This first-born son, who threatened to fall
    early from the womb,
Now struggles to free himself from home.
    Hunched over a book,
        ears closed to family,
    Knees drawn up,
        he continues his nativity.
Awash in hi-fi sound, he's shielded
    from a hostile world,
And from square corners of parents
    abrasive to his soul.

HAIKU

Almond eyes flash joy
    as two words unite two worlds...
        a good translation.

QUARREL

We are with each other as brittle
    as yesterday's toast.
Your irascible crust
    scratches my eardrums...

Silently across the table
    I implore:
Butter me with soft words, Beloved,
    or I crumble.

STOCKPILING

By the window sewing buttons against the cold,
The corner of her eye catches a plump squirrel
Stowing nuts to last the winter's span.

In the panelled room under the rug by the hearth
The family dog tucks a gnawed beef knuckle
Stealthily, as her ancestors must have saved
Against the hunt when no prey would fall.

Hauling groceries another day the housewife,
With something extra in case of storm,
Passes the Andrews Arsenal, and feels
Herself cringe and quiver as soldiers
Tuck the warheads gently underground.

SOUNDS IN AN EMPTY HOUSE

The dialogue is between
    furnace and refrigerator,
        set against each other:
            heat against cold...

Stressful joints creak
    as pines sough by roof,
        and embers grow grey...

Listen!

Could that be a key in the lock?
    A hand upon the door?

BLESSED BALM

We met at the fabric shop,
You buying remnants of velvet
   to frame your thoughts-in-oil,
I looking for thread to let down
   last year's hem. . .

Your glance framed my feelings,
Your touch rubbed smooth a lump,
Your words stitched up a wound. . .

O, salve,
O, ointment,
O, blessed balm of friendship!

GOOD NEIGHBORS

Your light illumines dark woods
   and marks paths we've trod,
      padding through underbrush;

Your light sniffs at boundaries,
   presses ever outward,
      gaps the sacred circle,
         probes the further darkness. . .

As time's stick strikes our hoops,
   past stone, and root,
      brier, and branch,
Feet seek flickers of light
   which sparkle the shadowed path. . .

Hands find the guiderope.

TOSS-AWAY DAY

Someday we must clean out this cupboard. . .
   . . .someday soon we'll organize,
      like on a Wednesday, because
   the trash man comes on Thursday. . .

We'll make a mound of our debris:
   The dreams that never fit the frame;
   The hopes that spoiled in storage;
   The ugly words that cracked in quarrels;
   The days we wasted in good intentions. . .

      And all the years not good enough to save. . .

BLACK HORSE

Terror rims the bulging eye, and
    pride drains from the nostrils
        as the snapped bones angle away
           from the blue-ribbon body,
              and
The crowd's roar groans
    into the silence
        of an empty stall.

FEAR FOR THE GENTLE

Fear for the gentle of the earth
For they shall be flattened
Under the caterpillar treads;
And they shall carpet the earth
In shades of beet-red and yellow,
For they lack conviction
To spring back, upright,
From the mower's blade.

IT'S HARD TO BE DIFFERENT BEFORE 11 P.M.

Say, did you ever stay up all night,
    having pretended to turn in
        with the rest of the family?

But your churning mind was too noisy for sleep,

So you wandered the house. . .from kitchen. . .
    to bath. . .to basement. . .
And finally parked in the STUDY,

Where you might have *studied*,
    had there not been a mirror on the wall,
        bevel-edged, and all,

Which put you in a traffic rotary,
    when what you really wanted was OUT. . .
A wide EXIT to a new town
    where the charter allows
        particularity. . .

Like, say, if you want to raise chickens
    in your backyard,
And I want to practice the flute,
We're free to try
    to *synchronize*. . .

And wouldn't that be lovely, and all-wise,
Your cock crowing well on his heap o' dung,
And I rejoicing with loud flute notes,
    sincerely *flung*!

SAMPLES

When people refer to me as a poet,
I wonder if they want to see a sample?
Or hear me breathe vocal life into silent ink?

It's as if they're saying,
"She's a diabetic;"   or "She's a bleeder;"
So when I go for a check-up,
    the technician says,
"Give us, please, a sample," and
Points me toward the private door,
    where, alone with my gods and devils,
    I let go the hoarded waste into the cup,

To be whirled through the centrifuge,
    trickled through the computer,
And discreetly handed to the physician,
    who translates the hieroglyphs to say,
"It's good;"   or "It's no good;"
    or "It's somewhere inbetween;"

And I accept the fact that in
    these sloughed-off cells,
    these metabolized emotions,
These telltale words dried upon the page,
    are inscribed forever
The pathology of a phase.

THE SECOND SEASON

Cicadas saw in contrapuntal rhythm
    as sprinklers arc over lilac and leaves,
        and trickles of water snake underground.

Flashes of firefly yellow belie caution. . .
    guitar notes fall in casual caress. . .

A cyclist's arabesques on the macadam
    draw from a nubile girl loud applause,
And dogs from house to house are startled
    into anxious dialogue.

The cyclist's older brother, with one-armed aplomb,
    wheels his rod around the corner,
        blending exhaust with sweet petunia
            and acrid marigold.

The housebound Burmese cat peers from the crossbeam
    into the wooded darkness beyond her wall of glass,

And you and I move out to the hammock
    under the dogwood canopy;

Beside the August-green poinsettia
    we sway in humid air,
        framed in moonbeams,
            bracketed by time. . .
                easing through the second season. . .

JOY UPSHAW MURPHY

Joy Murphy was born in Memphis, Tennessee, but grew up and had her early schooling in Florida and Mississippi. High school years found her in Memphis once again where she later graduated from Southwestern University with a Bachelor of Music degree.

Mrs. Murphy is married to a law professor at the University of North Carolina and has three sons. She teaches piano and sings and writes.

FREEDOM TO GO

Twelve years ago we crossed with the light,
Sun and excitement glinted in your eyes
And I held your small hand tight—there
On your first day to school.

Tonight, we walked across the campus,
Your hand enveloped mine; then turning
Your tall frame against the street lights,
There was a reflection caught in your eye,
But quickly wiped away—
Lingering that moment, you seemed aware.

AFTER HEARING "THE SEVENTH TRUMPET,"
BY DONALD ERB

You have good ears, Mr. Erb—
Sharp jags of blocked trumpets
Rip above the strings,
Drums roll with motor sounds
Breaking the sky,
Timpani lap through water—
Displaced reeds blow sighs—
Mourns, wails, screams
Collide with the flute,
The trumpets' and strings' glissando
Whisper in glossolalia
Begging for death.
No comedy here; cacophony
We know—not music, not beauty,
How you sound like us!
Your apocalypse is scary as Revelations,
You hear too well, Mr. Erb, the warning
Sounds of the Scripture—
Oh, to return to the "Rite of Spring"!

IN MEMORY OF GARY STEIN
(Whom his friends called Captain Yi)

11:30 P.M., December, 1974, New Haven

Walking free in happiness,
Always, "The Captain's" long strides had marked each step,
Now, anxious to arrive, for Lynn is waiting
Waiting—
Then—
Colder than the sidewalk, Lynn's fear freezes;
Waiting at the hospital, stunned friends bow over—

Hoping—wishing—praying;
Oh, God, he had crawled sixty feet,
Trying so hard to reach somewhere—
His stomach hollowed out on the street;
That sawed-off shotgun gutted him—
Mind, ambition, life crashed
Forever.

Leaving to the world those twisted two
Who never knew him
Who never could care to reach
Anywhere.

SON, NUMBER TWO

How quickly you fell from the womb
When you came into the world—
You explored the top of everything
Falling many times—
You never minded the hurt
Nor stopped the climb!

Now, off to college,
There's only one pair of cutoffs left
Otherwise your floor is empty—
How odd, that I should miss the clutter!
I pick them up, rocking them,
Wanting a scent of you, and
Hating to wash you farther away!

Back from college—
It's so much fun to have you home!
Why must you again leave so soon?
Restless, it's been too long?
You must avoid this smothering—
Go—then—don't feel guilty—
I, too, must go—to my new environment.

THE MISSING LINK

I am among Them
Surrounded by their newness
And seeing them do their thing
I am the stranger, the used up,
Unable to look through their colors—
Their words, I know, but not their connotation,
Sounds of notes, but my soul does not move,
I sit alone, a minority generation now
As the sea of youth merges with its sudden
Melting into the screen, becoming the 2001 scene.

THE WAITING ROOM

Many times I opened the heavy door
For your stumbling steps, and no longer perfect eyes,
You've sat in these chairs
Anxiously—impatiently—
At the doctor's office.
Wanting to be examined by all—
M.D.s, podiatrists, oculists, dentists—
A revolving search in hope.
Now, I'm here alone
No longer the weight on my arm—
I miss your presence today.

RAIN

Rain soaks into skin
Chills away all inside warmth—
I push through the pouring
Step into the puddles—
I rush inside
Wanting you.

THE FLIGHT

Yesterday you walked into the sky,
Looked down at earth and river, moving slowly:
Did you think? "She will go up through the mountainous white
And join with me this free bird feeling of winging through the bright."
And then, remembering, say, "I've felt this way before—
Not in a plane—just with her."
If you could think these thoughts,
I need not question more.

INSIDE LOOKING OUT

Stretched along limb with fat and fur hanging over
Eyes half closed to smarting wind,
Tail curled over for warmth and balance
The grey squirrel digs into the bark,
Soaks up the sun preparing for
A long winter buried in a brown nest.
Through the storm window, I see
Small birds dart from bare branch to tree trunk,
Looking thinner with so few bugs,
And working frantically on the surface to find one.
In the mirror I clean, black trees
Stripped of all their dressing,
Skeleton against the sky.
A lonely wasp lazy from the cold
Weakly buzzes against its red reflection.
I focus on the mirror's images and wonder
What will be the winter's toll?

OXFORD, MISSISSIPPI

Confederate soldier standing there
Again and again you must die—
As you did fighting for this court square,
Where you now are honored or despised.

You, who thinking you fought for your home and land,
Died a victim of political shortsightedness—
You, who did not want secession or war,
Were needlessly used to uphold words—
Spoken by others in haste, pride and greed for power,
Which sent you all the way to Gettysburg
And home again, dead.

SEA EMBRACE

Awake, I lift up to see
Ripening sea oats
Lean over mounds of sand,
Which underfoot stretch a border of gold
And slide into the pellucid water,
Doubling the lone egret and
Its jade green grass retreat.

My eyes walk from lagoon to beach;
They squint at the frothy roll
Beating the shore—
Its changing tide washing clean
The earth's bottom.

Soon I lie looking up at green filigreed blue,
Encircled by thin fences of green,
Relief comes to an aching void; is filled
With the heavy wave's pounding rise and fall.
Late in the day, I see again a lagoon,
Serene, reaching up to a setting sun
Millions of tiny drops of light
Blinding reason with their fire.

Out of the dark, the moon
Sinks soft satin
Completing oblivion
To tomorrow.

LET US SEE, FLOWER CHILDREN

How indignant we are that you should flaunt tradition,
And thus slap us in the face with your weird and open
    rejection!
Can we admit we sowed and now reap this adamant desertion?
That we are the ones who twisted our own life,
And in the spiritual failure to meet our strife,
We took the beautiful dreams and ideals from men of vision,
Scoffed, doubted, hesitated, dissected their usefulness
In a mechanized, modern penicillin world.
Oh, we manipulated social reform and clung to somewhat
    approved formality
Trying to enrich modern man materialistically!
Even long ago a "nature boy in a park" did not deter
    our loss of soul and individuality,
And the whole generation in its hurry and rush, proceeded
    in oblivion to his prognostic warnings—
Until now, we are surrounded by you, the actively passive
    "flower children,"
Who see no hope in our empty, soulless, confusing example
And point to the failure of a people who inherited everything,
But like spoiled children used nothing constructively.
Is it too late to lift our eyes from a mad, torn world
    of false sophistication
Which you are seeking desperately, perhaps unintentionally,
    to portray,
And believe again in One Source of constant beauty in one
    lovely tree or flower
Before it and we fall victim to complete annihilation and decay?

BARBARA ROWAN

Barbara Rowan was born in San Francisco, California and was educated in music at Mills College in Oakland. She spent a year in Paris as a Fulbright Scholar under Darius Milhand. As a pianist, she has appeared with the San Francisco and Oakland Symphony Orchestras and has performed extensively as a soloist and chamber music artist in North Carolina and neighboring states. She is presently on the teaching faculty at the University of North Carolina, is married and has a daughter and a son.

She began writing poetry in college and later wrote more intensively while living in Chapel Hill. She writes to discover, and making poems has become for her a transforming way of orienting herself to the physical world and to the human experience in which the poem itself is a symbol of participation.

POEMS

Poems come with dignity
            not to be coerced
            under the pen
quietly
from the deep places
like an odor from a working kitchen

CHRISTOPHER ROBIN, THE NEW
AFTER PANTRY PLAY

Onions on his feet
walking into Washington
he takes his wooden sword
and strikes down ten senators
who stand against
Bears

In their stubborn blood
he presses his toes
and asks if his relief
has added any new joys to
Bearhood

AFTER THE WAR

It is easier
to love
when all our hate
is served to the enemy
in a gun
or a protest banner...

Later
we must try to love
in the midst of those
unnamed feelings
we all have
which try to destroy

SNOW

Snow is a killer of time
Molded arrester of movement

Snow is a suffocator
Ice brilliant lock

Snow is a binder
Stiffened trapper
Still confiner

Falling frozen
Snow is a surprised statue
An oversharp candid Beauty
Beguiler

Silent sound-muter
Unmotioned force
Beckoner

A near cruel breath-stealer
Ender

Snow is a sign
Factual dogma
Holy attention-getter
Event

HERE WE ARE

In simple motion

the sea fish drop to near ground

looking
and scurrying

beneath the

heavy tide

Drawing closer

the sea wall drowns and thunders

Roars
in devilish divisions

sounding like curled music, fish

tossed within its folds

easily

largely:

Here we are

small eyes in sounding foam

swimming

LIFE DANCERS

                              Slowly
we straighten round
come to the snow place
to the near ground
                              spreading
        like narrow fans to take air

We
        folded pictures
        seen on a side by light
                              on a side
        half open
                  drifting by night

                                        figures
                                        flowers
                                        wheels
        form ourselves

                  so darkly
                  so blackly

        before the closing

        before the flakes take flight

POEMS FOR NICKLE AND DAN

How do birds swim?
Feathered arms fan
A dark
Liquid
Surface

How do snakes fly?
Coiled in a measured
Highlight:
Leap!

How do dogs read?
Looking up to a
Loving reference:
Infer

How do cats work?
Searching in slim
Loveliness
For a frame:
Repose

How do dragons tease?
Eating ice on flaming
Tongues:
Cool approach

How do rabbits snarl?
Long teeth
On shortening lettuce

HALLOWED EVENING

I saw
Hallowe'en in Colony Woods
pasted on the doors

The children had heard ghostly tales
at camp
in the streets
in sunny schools

Their familiarity with spirits
from fighting night
gives them bright mischief
as if the spirits had caught them up
for their own team

Throwing up designs for passersby
jolly ghouls
orange frights
sweet witches in kindergarten
ask for favors
buying one more year's time
against the mighty trickster

All souls bob for more time
more light

DAY LILIES

Somewhere
deep in recesses sheltering a thoughtful voice
an urge
striving for definition
tries to shape a union between my eye and
what it sees

It is a question

and light
a mysterious partner
coming and going
fixes the moments of pursuit
outlining the temporal with its holy quality

changing it
changing us

like the day lilies
being born and dying
in their limited quantity of glory

WOODSTOCK

I thought about feelings
half the night
and wondered about crowds
at Woodstock
      hanging about
      unidentified
      in mystery units and tents

I suppose
I could take a guitar
and ask them
in ten languages
anything
but the right thing
            (nudely and rudely)

"Your hair, Miss Pomeroy,
crosses your belly button
in the nicest way. . ."

but that would never do
since it doesn't matter
and she left her
last name
somewhere
back in the violet woods
where the clouds
sweep the treetops for housekeeping

She,
blinking long-eyed
not solemnly
but only five times
in one minute
has nothing to say to me

She eats berries
when she has time
from the ground

tunelessly
in the midst of a sound
that would crush your insides

each berry sliding down
an unfamiliar route
of foreign compounds
brushing against
acid
speed
grass
and very long hyphenated monstrosities
that old toe wrigglers like me
shudder to pronounce

I have stopped too
to go way inside
and in a way
I suppose her trip is part of my luggage;
she sits there
inside me
cross legged
much more Yoga advanced
than I
and exists behind my eyes
like a blank angel

HAZEL F. THOMAS

Hazel F. Thomas looked back on some of the poems she wrote more than 25 years ago and decided to try her hand at writing again. After all, she reasoned, heritage means a lot to most people—memories, things to ponder, in other words, the stuff of which poetry is made. A member of the North Carolina Poetry Society, the Friday Noon Poetry Club in Chapel Hill, and the Sand Leaf Writers Club in Sanford, North Carolina, Mrs. Thomas attends classes in creative writing at Sandhills Community College and Carolina Technical Institute in Sanford.

Mrs. Thomas is a native of Sanford where she lives with her husband and son. She also has two married daughters.

DUEL

Slender necks
stretch in a militant arch
Dull cones
turn scarlet
Ebony wings lift
to fence with a white leg-horn
Cocks dive
in whirlwind of chaff and feathers
Deep spur-galled wounds
spurt blood
Beaks pinch
swollen cones bruising dark purple
The victor
withdraws dripping spurs
with black breast bone pushed high
He pecks stubble from wounds
Marbled white feathers
lie still
in vivid sunlight—

MINDS MEET

From my house
by the side of the road
Like the grasp
of a hand
I felt the warm spirit
of two truck drivers
reach across the yellow line
as they met
going in the opposite direction
No rubber duck
No ten-four
needed
Eighteen wheelers—

MY TURN

The wells
were low on that farm day long ago
My five brothers
were not home when Papa
called my name
Excited
I waited by the barn door
for him to help me mount Pet
the mare he raised from a colt
I felt his pride
as he watched me ride bare-back
to a clear spring
Pet drank
and saw me in the water
She did not care
that
I
was
a
girl—

WAR

We can dress it up
and thrill to military bands
soldiers in dress parade
marching feet

With old glory
gallantly streaming
Underneath the brave songs
clicking heels
and shining brass

War is
havoc, confusion a holocaust
With goodbyes drowned out
by a war train whistle
Eyes blurring salt-tears
millions dying
paying the price for what is right
and sometimes wrong

War was heart-break for my family
when three brothers left home
to serve
in Sicily
in Normandy
the Philippines
the fourth brother training for battle

The taxi brought the telegram
while hearts froze
Dad assuring Mother
"only wounded in battle"
as she choked
"which one?"

BOND OF MUSIC

He had four fiddles
Playing for me he said

"I knew the first time
I pulled the bow across
the strings I would buy it
Shucks
all it needed was a new
set of steel strings
Some good resin
for the bow"

Remembering age fourteen
the challenge of a fiddle
in his hands
The fiddle bond grew
between father and son

Today
he can play any tune
you can name—

BILLY

On my lap at age four
he pushed my arms saying
"I don't need a seat belt"
Mom's cue to pull back

We dared not touch even then
toy cars in parked formation
Enjoyed boyhood dreams
inventive mind

Sixteen now
a time of hero worship
soaring ego
and silent moods

I ache for him
waiting for the bridge of union
Long to touch
man, little boy
but remember
no seat belt—

COUNTRY WALK

By the garden path
I waited
knowing she would pass this way
The sainted lady with the kind face
and white hair
Who could blow fire out of burns
tie up a sore toe
Once in a vision—
she saw brother Frank in heaven
Skipping along I listen to her
sweet gentle voice
The country road, its half mile to
her mail box winds through tall pines
Looking straight up I could see sky
Two crows flying
Fox hounds tired from early hunt
ignored the big stick in her hand
On bare toes I could see inside her
mail box
Cloverine salve—
To my burn it felt cool
Blurting out my fear of thunder
She prayed,
"Please God, in storms take care of
little girls."
With brother Frank now—
our neighbor
who could blow fire out of burns. . .

PHYSIOGNOMY

I have heard the story
all of my life
about a little fellow
who ran a mile
on his fourth birthday

Brought home kicking—
Tied in a chair
against his will
before a black curtain
draped over a box
with tall legs

Glass shutters
clicked an image
dressed in a home-made
Eton suit

The story
does not tell anything
Only I
see the sad expression
quiver of lips
in Papa's photograph—

PET

We raised
and loved a little colt
Pet—
She was a team in one
and seemed to know
our livelihood
depended on her

One morning
we felt the hush
as men gathered quietly
around the old barn

Mom kept us
in the house for a while
Standing by the window
she wiped her eyes
with the corner of her apron
and no one talked much

Days later
we walked through woods
to uncle Paul's house
On the way we stopped
and stood for a while
by a big grave—

LONE AQUATOT

Barely old enough
to leave the back yard
I crawled under barbed wire
slipped past
staring eyes of fenced cows

Familiar shouts
drew me
like an iron magnet
skinny dipping
into waist deep water
to where a shovel lay
on a damned up creek bank

Shocked brothers
splashed out
grappled with buddies
for scattered blue denim

fled home to Mom
who scolded
Great Scots alive!

PINE STORY

Pine trees glisten
        over pine-barren land
Summer breezes
      bend long needles in unison
Blowing sound of hidden music

Cone clusters drop quietly
          on brown straw below
A buzz saw hums far away

    Trees fall

Grinding gears shift to low
      The battered truck disappears
Its heavy load of trees stripped
      but for big log chains

Winds drift
        sweet smell of pine

AN ACT OF LOVE

Walking slowly toward
his little shop
Uncle Will could barely
see the path through
unshed tears

Family members
failed to persuade him
to change his mind—

To carry out his sister's
request would only
deepen the sorrow

"I must get on with it"
he choked
"because she asked me to"

All day and far into the night
he worked
Grief knitting his heart
in an act of love

The mahogany coffin
was made for my grandmother
Margaret Wicker Foushee
in nineteen twenty-two—

SOARING

Climb on
ambitious mind
Nature within
wonders through
hours which
are not here
Hungering for
things above
Soaring higher
toward regions
unknown
Creating images
of great things
to come —

KATE KELLY THOMAS

Kate Kelly Thomas is a native Tarheel who, after her five children were grown, went back to school, studying creative writing at Sandhills Community College in Southern Pines, North Carolina. An active member of the North Carolina Poetry Society, Mrs. Thomas also divides her time between the North Carolina Extension Homemakers and writing groups in the central Carolina area. She and her husband live on their strawberry farm near Sanford, North Carolina.

SALOME

Take it away
blood seeps yet
beneath his chin.
Repugnant eyes stare
from the platter
  chilling me.
Take it away. . .take my food
  I gag!
  (such a head of hair)
Let me mime some other
uncomplicated affair. Forget
my dance, my song and me,
blame my mother. . . .

INTENSIVE CARE

"FAMILY MEMBERS MAY VISIT
THE FIRST FIVE MINUTES OF
EACH HOUR."

Center of my Universe
"KNOCK AND WAIT FOR NURSE"
Earth pivots as the long hand
dashes from twelve to one.
Shaping to sick-beds
and hospital smells
I return to the long waiting room
sit on a straight chair
among strangers,
and eclipse their talk
slip-stitch their talk
with a red crochet hook
and yarn,
rust and beige.

AFRAID TO KNOW

The tractor was standing idle
although it was far away
I sensed something. . .very wrong
by the way he lay. I strained
to see, then hurried there
my heart was filled with fright,
his twisted head. . .hand over eyes
as if to shield them from light.

His wrench was near one rigid hand.
That stillson was opened wide!
The plow that he had used it on
was tilted by his side. My heart
pounded faster, my feet
slowed their pace,
I bent toward him slowly
I had to see his face.

WHEN GRANDPA WATCHED FROM THE HILL

The hill between his house
and mine. . .
Mount Everest for a girl
who was four. Grandpa
would say, "I'll walk to the top
then watch you through your door."
    He'd turn loose my hand. . .
    I'd go down the dirt road
    as brave as I could be
    but ever so often I stopped—
    Looked back.
    To make sure he was looking
    at me.
Tall as the tallest pine!
His bond. . .true as its roots.
He lifted all fright from the girl
of four 'till she waved from
her Mother's door.

MY TURN TO WATCH

He turned loose my hand and made a fist
when the great pain came
so tight his nails left prints.
I remembered tender giant hands
as I watched by his bed. . .
calmed again his groping hands.
This rawboned man lashed out. . .
his tall wooden bed
was, "Too damn short."
The nights were, "Too damn long."
  We eased his long frame crossways
  and promised the light would come soon.

TOBACCO AUCTION

Fity-big-five fity-big-five fix-six
seben-ma heben-pa who-pa oo-ma eight
ate-de-biddy ate-de-biddy who-nine
do-nine nine-a-hine nine-a-hine
fity-nine- 'ollars---------------'Merican!

Red shirted Auctioneer
fist overhead
plows through rows of sheeted tobacco
calling bids above the roar
of farm trucks, tow motors, warehouse jargon.
Buyers wipe sweat and dust
while Farmers grin at their good sale
or cuss that P-G grade!
Sweet rank tobacco odors
spill into the street
drawing red necks and stragglers
who come to swap yarns
to feel the silky leaf
and to listen. . .

Fity-big-five fity-big-five fix-six
seben-ma heben-pa who-pa oo-ma eight
ate-de-biddy ate-de-biddy who-nine
do-nine nine-a-hine nine-a-hine
fity-nine- 'ollars-----------------'Merican.

KATYDID CULTURE

Pretty baby, grow a tooth, learn to walk
Katydid, Katydid.
Good grades, compete, stand straight
play games, have fun
Katydid.
Grow up, car, career, marry, have fun
Katydid, Katydid.
Settle down, buy a house, family
get ahead, save money
Katydid.
Bigger house, more cars, more fun
vacations
Katydid, Katydid.
Retire, retire, think more
play more, have fun
then die, then die
Katydid.

BETTER NIGHTS

I've known better nights—
nights you told me, with your
special look, "I am yours."
Tonight you ignore me to
flirt with some other.
Cut me short with a tongue
so recently sharpened—
Put me down with your arrogant wit
to amuse our party friends,
and going home. . .a silence
so thick I can feel it.
    Lights out and you think
    with your holy body, you can
    right a ruined evening,
    stay a stained relationship,
    salve a shattered universe.

THIS DAY IS DIFFERENT

This day is different
your eyes refuse to meet mine.
I miss your image
over my shoulder
as I brush my hair.
       Your tight lips
       speak volumes. . .
       your coffee, absorbing.
       Mine, tasteless.

Do you remember
when the sharing stopped?
When I turned my cheek
as you sought my lips?
When you left the room
and my voice dropped. . . .

SYMPATHIZING

We speak simple things. . .
rain that didn't come until
the hay was mowed,
a new highway dividing our land.
　　Words falter
　　you are David
　　he. . . Absalom.
They place coffee in your hand,
"Sugar and cream?"
"Yes, no. . .I mean black."
Mary tells of a school play
the tone is light,
and Mr. Luke celebrated
his ninety-first birthday.
　　An Egyptian Mother
　　no blood on my door.
Martha's pies won three blue ribbons
at the State Fair. . . .
　　Friends are sometimes kind
　　supposing the hurt will ease
　　if we speak
　　simple things.

UNDERSTANDING

"Looks lak I'm gonna have to whup
them okras."
My eyes questioned him.
"Too many green leaves
keeps 'em from bearing."
My smile was tolerant of this plant
of African origin.
    I saw his method.
    Between sunset and dark
    he 'whupped' the okra
    with a branch
    from the pecan tree.
Three days later he was at my door
grinning a peck of tender pods.
I nodded seeingly at this man
of African origin.

POETRY

No more will I wrestle time
nor hoard the favorite
day, nor drop my
anchor in
stagnant
pools.
I'll sail in moving waters
metering all things
by poetry
called
life.

FRIEND

He cannot live his life without a lust.
They say to him, "You are not much a man."
And always do they show their great disgust,
I am a friend and I will give my trust.

His mind, his body goes the way of rust,
Rebukes: "You do not use your gifts, what shame!"
I am a friend and I will give my trust.

We live our lives. We will return to dust,
Unless I show, how will he ever know
I am a friend and I will give my trust.

CURE FOR INSOMNIA

I bought a book of poetry
thirteen eighty nine!
That's a lot of money
sixty cents per line!
Comes a night that I can't sleep
I appreciate its worth,
what these poems do for me
beats anything on Earth.
These few words are priceless
their meaning. . .so deep,
I read for seven minutes
and promptly fall asleep.

MARSHA WHITE WARREN

Marsha White Warren, born in Middletown, Ohio, in 1938 and raised in Dayton, graduated from Miami University in Oxford, Ohio, with a B.S. in education in 1960. The move to North Carolina came with her husband's admission to Duke Law School in Durham, and she began her teaching career in local schools. After stops in London and Washington, she and her family have settled in Chapel Hill, North Carolina.

Mrs. Warren's interest in poetry has been longtime in her love for the writings of Robert Frost and Beatrix Potter, but in 1978 she began writing poetry herself, as the most positive vehicle for dealing with her mother's death six months earlier. She has found that poetry has "opened up a part of me I hadn't known needed wing."

IT'S ME

Don't expect from me
Reactions formulated
In *your* mind, when
I meet a situation
I must ponder.

Don't press on for comment
To inquiry, smile or phrase
When it's premature
For me to répondez.

We try to clinch involvement
From passers by in life
When there's a need to
Stand back and observe.

So let me make my
Statement, show my hand
And ante up, when
I feel inspired, and
Then you'll know it's me.

HIDING PLACE

I saw a hiding place today.
A nook, a cranny, a niche.
So hidden away, I wanted to hide there
But I didn't need a place.

Not today, not now.
I said, "I'll remember the spot
And someday it would be
Waiting for me."

But you can't save hiding places,
Stash them away in your mind
For a time you need them.

The very nature of a hiding place
Is the spontaneity of it.
And it can be any place that's right
For the time.

And if you looked at it later
You'd say it didn't look thought out.

But times you need to hide,
Be by yourself—alone—apart,
The place need only be there
Welcoming you to its privacy.

POET'S PURPOSE

It was nothing unusual
That I took Frost with me.
I'd been taking him along for years.

Where I got the book and when, I can't recall.
It's paper back and easy to pack
And as the years went along, I got the "works"
But it's not the same as the dog-eared one.

The world Frost saw, he recorded.
I read his recollections
And now I try to write
My life's impressions.

So on this trip I took my friend,
I took him along to my mother's side.
To comfort me? To comfort her?

Proudly, she said when the reading was done,
She'd never felt smart enough
To understand the words of poets.
And I was glad I'd erased those fears.

There's a purpose for poets in this world.
We don't always know what it is.
And the sense makes sense
When we're least expecting it.
But the wisdom speaks to us
When we're ready to hear it.

I'm glad I took Frost with me that trip,
To see my mother for the last time.
But I wasn't aware I'd taken the book.
It was just there when I needed it.

"THANK YOU AUDEN FOR ALBEE"

The arm thrust out and in the hand
Were sheets of poems which bore
The soul of a young man.

Such bold audaciousness
To hand untested words
To masters!

The side that clutched while
Waiting for the open door
Was smudged with sweat and
Curled with doubt.

"Would you please, Sir, read my poems,
I'll return in two weeks time."
There! The words were out. Back
Down the steps—don't look. Flee!

Returns to find a playwright he should be.

EVEN ROOT CELLARS CAN BURN

Her possessions were expressions.
Impressions of her life and
Of the lives of those departed.
The twinkle in her eyes
When a treasure was discovered,
Reground, repaired and placed
With utmost care, was beauty to behold.
Her work of art, her home.
Her insides on display.
Destroyed in half an hour
Like the time we spend pre-Christmas
Then with lightning speed undo.
"Faulty wiring," they said.
As if it sanctioned
The disaster, the exposure of
A side she'd let us see.
Would she be as eager next time
To be so honest in this "faulty" world?

BUT I DIDN'T SEE IT!

Each day
As Spring draws closer,
Movement occurs.
Hardly recognizable
Barely perceptible.
And the only way
We can be sure
Movement occurs,
Is that the bare
Brown branches
Are green with fluff and
Up from the soil
A daffodil
Salutes the sun.

THISTLES

Thistles reaching toward the sky
In purple skirts
Though upside down
They look straight up,
A gallant try.

The purple part is so inviting
It looks of feather soft.
A bit of down
A cottonball
The hue is quite enticing.

But when your eager hand it reaches
To pluck a few
For Winter's vase,
A clever name the thistle has
The stabbing lesson teaches.

AN OLD FRIEND

I chanced to see a friend tonight
I hadn't seen for years.
I caught his glance across the room,
Such memories—near to tears.

His hair was grey
His beard the same
I thought how strange
This life—a game.

For his son's the one I often see
Now here it was the dad,
And sure as I was standing there
The face I'd known, his son now had.

"Hello, how nice to see you,"
How long can it have been.
So many thoughts were flooding
How old were we back then?

It must have been a long time
In school and taking classes.
And as I write these words down
I, too, am grey—with glasses.

NOT POSSIBLE

I never thought it possible
To live without my mother.
Someone who's been the
Root of me, the heart of me,
Not possible.

How can one be motherless?
Many are I know
But I couldn't bear the thought
To be without my mother.
Not possible.

But death takes all and her too soon.
Snatched away before my eyes.
My world fell in—I *do* live on
And realize now she's *not* gone.
Not possible.

OF EQUAL IMPORTANCE

What's the step from Frost to me?
From reading to writing?
It warms me, calms me
Expresses my thoughts as
Effectively now as then.

But the reading's not done.
It's there to replenish
Refurbish, renew.
It's my buffer
To the outside world.

JAMAICA

Delicate children. Beautiful!
And smiles that shine in their eyes.
Gentle baby goats near to mother's full breasts.
The quietest cries you're bound to hear.
The boldest in sea and wind.

Fireflies and crickets light up the night
As brilliantly as the stars shine
Their messages of distance and form,
And the familiar groups of stars
Are upside down and out of phase.

Color, sight, sound, black!
More black than you've ever seen and
White would be wrong 'mongst the
Palms and plants, baskets and beads.
"Real coral, Mon!"

We're here to rest in a land *of* rest,
In a land *at* rest.
By the sea, in the sea, on the sea
And the rum runs free.
How long can we be leisure?

JAMAICAN HOLIDAY

The sun is free for all to use
The water's for all to drink.
The ground sends forth food for everyone
Who sows and reaps.

But life isn't always as fair
As Mother Nature is.
Men differ drastically in mind
And opportunity.

I seek a bright sun on holiday.
The folks here would be
Happy for cold.
But I am the advantaged one.

So I can see their sun
They don't see mine.
I eat their food
Mine, they'll never know.

I drink their rum
They can't afford Scotch.
I taste their life
But it's not *their* life I feel.

I don't make baskets
I buy them.
I don't cook the food
I eat it.

I don't toil in the heat
I bask in the sun.
I fly home in the end.
They are chained to the isle.

But the sun is free for all to use
The water's for all to drink
And the ground sends forth food for everyone
Who sows and reaps.

HELEN BEATRIX POTTER

"Please Cox!
Just one small mouse.
The pantry has enough
To spare. Just one. Oh Please!"
The guarded smile
Upon the butler's face
Assured to this small
Plain and lonely child
A little friend who'd
Help his mistress pass
The time—the time,
The endless time
Alone in nursery top.

Did old Cox live to
See what he'd begun
With this frail child?
Did he see genius grow,
The pets increase, the scraps
And snips of pictures change to
Tiny little books?
Those tiny little books for
Tiny hands to hold.
Exquisite drawings, so alive
The flowers smelled, the
Attics creaked and that mouse
Running by with the cradle. . . .looks REAL!

BY DAY

By day, the folks look on
And chills run up their spines
As watching from afar
See chests quite bare, backs of brawn
Lower with each shovelful
'Til only the dirt can now be seen
Twirling up and out on air,
Takes flight and scatters
To the winds.

By passing on or standing still
The living assuredly attest
The hole is not for them.
The dirt flies up 6 feet on top,
The church bell rings, 'tis 6 o'clock.
Now deep enough, the
Straining crawl toward
Light and freedom up above,
Those men who don their
Shirts and brush their brow
Must wonder at their deed
As if they are in league
With evil waves that bring
A man down to his grave.
For on the morrow at 6 am
The dirt will go in place again.

But by night, the soul of man now
In this earthly home
Takes flight and scatters
To the stars.

MARCH 17

These were Sally's flowers
They've been moved from her side to mine.
But they'll always be hers.
It's one year today she left.

She was nearly gone in body
When we talked about our plan
But her mind was sharp
And eager for the scheme.

"I've got it," I said,
"The solution for the iris
To relieve the crowding
On your side of the fence.

Since your mums grow through
To my side
Let's just plant them where they go
So they'll have a place
That they can call their own."

So carefully the small shoots were moved.
And they flourished and bloomed.
Though she never saw them then
I know she sees them now.

Her love and spirit moved through that fence.
Her life touched mine and lasts.
And in the Fall, fireworks of color
Testify the pact.

Each March when I clear away the deadwood
And see below the fresh green shoots,
I recall the day I said to her,
"Sally, I have a plan.
Let's move the plants from your side to mine."
And her smile lit up my life.

NINA A. WICKER

Nina Apple Wicker was born on a family farm in Caswell County and has been writing since second grade but not seriously until the 1970s when *Farm Journal, Inc.* published an article she had written about a neighbor. Since then Mrs. Wicker has seen her work published in *Miscellany, The Progressive Farmer,* the North Carolina *Christian Advocate, Country Living, Pegasus, Pembroke Magazine, The Sanford Herald, Parnassus, Cairn,* and *Dragonfly.* An active member of the North Carolina Poetry Society, she was listed in 1977 and 1978 in *International Who's Who in Poetry.* Mrs. Wicker has studied with Page Shaw, Sam Ragan, Sharon Shaw and Julian Long. She resides in Sanford with her family.

STOP THE WORLD, I WANNA GET OFF

on a ferris wheel gone wild
catching blurred glimpses of a milling crowd
swinging loose at the top
daring to be dumped
straining to focus a familiar face,
I choke back sickness
and start to wave frantically
knowing all the while
a grease-dipped lever pusher
will think I'm an adult kid
in this for the ride.

SECOND SEMESTER

from the family bathroom
to the room where he slept
he carried the toiletries
placing each item carefully in his satchel
    ...never saying a word
he blow-dried his hair
unplugged the drier
slowly and painstakingly wrapped up the cord
we sat
watching, waiting
    ...never saying a word
he slipped bare feet into sandals
casually picked up his sweat jacket
bow and arrow and brown paper bag
and the only words we knew to say were
    'goodbye and be careful'

THE FIRST TIME

the first time i felt
the warmth of your breath
i thought it was spring
and april was enticing me
to come
enjoy her showers
little did i know
that your velocity would increase
and i'd be forever trapped
in the eye of your storm

UNCLAIMED

stamped PREPAID
with dog-eared corners
i arrive at your door
requesting no re-wrap
just a quick opening
. . .an acceptance
without signature
guaranteed to last
beyond the warranty
that covers me

THUMBED

you taxied into my life
metered my every turn
passing on the wrong side
you whizzed me through the slums
not once did you slow down
or honk your horn
    —but thanks to a blow-out
today i lean on the bus sign
and wait another ride

SUNDAY MORNING TV

The boob tube blares directions
from every corner of this
    Wander-land.
Would-be prophets shout,
    Plant a seed!
    Let go and let God!
    Expect a miracle!
    Hang on to Jesus!
But, Lord,
something good happens to me
when I turn it off and
go outside and
listen to the birds.

STALKING

That wide-winged Bird
isn't a crow—
more like a hawk.
His indigo feathers
reflect the rainbow...
some say he knows
the whereabouts of the pot of gold!
The prey know He's flying around
    seeking whom He can devour
but they don't waste any time
watching for Him
—or running
    maybe it's just as well
the Record promises
only believers survive!

LIFE'S RIBBON

Life's ribbon runs taut
daily encounters checked off
. . .a grocery list
One day down
How many to go?
Happenings running from
before a slap on the rear
to after the last shovel of dirt
All an eternity—
a NOW track
with every man's ribbon
a circle.

IN HIS HAND

A calendar hangs
on the world's wall
advertising the neutron bomb
refuge stations, cloning
but the Real Manufacturer's
    Unsecret Agent
re-affirms in His Manual
. . .one day is as a thousand years. . .
and He
remains the same
yesterday, today and tomorrow

DEATH COMING

wire message
an accident
DEATH elbows in
for consideration
a terrible, hopeless, dark
    Mystery
but, Lord
help me remember Calvary. . .
and cry
"Oh, death, where (now)
is thy sting?"

MAP READING

On this cross-
road of life
North bound
man beckons
to my left and to my right
enticing me
to follow.
Keep me
from yielding,
Lord,
remembering. . .
You authorized
no detour sign!

BLACK-EYED SUSANS

When the painter pulls
his two-wheel brush
and divides the highway
with yellow lines
   some broken
   some solid
Does he know that year 'round
another Painter slowly
and painstakingly
is preparing the ditches
for a profusion of Fall Color
to match the ribbon lines
   some solid
   some broken

PROGRESS?

it hasn't always been
fields of concrete
    and clover leaf patches
mind film, though faded
    and now reeling too fast
records rolling hills
grain in its green
    and fields of clover
sometimes red

SUPPER

The breakfast of life
was meeting you.
No need for lunch
we rollicked through.
Our evening has slowed
our appetites gone.
When was supper
and where is Home?

AFTER THE SHADOWS

That day—
    The sun seeped through the falling shutters
    Crawled under the crack in the door
    Lowered itself through the hole in the roof
    and danced in lace shadows on a dusty old floor.
It played a symphony in the locks of my child
Warmed the crocuses right out of the ground.
Melted the ice on matted pine needles
And moved creeks to running under sheets of ice.
That same day—
    It burst my heart
    Unveiled my eyes
    Oiled my bearings
    And switched my life to GO!

BRENDA LOY WILLIAMSON-PRATT

Brenda Loy Williamson-Pratt has received favorable recognition in the Carolinas for her poetry. A native of Alamance County in North Carolina, she lives in Burlington where she also works as a secretary and bookkeeper. Active in the Burlington Writer's Club, she has received recognition in their annual Spring Writer's Festival over the last five years for her poetry, children's stories, and drama. She has been published in *Maggie's Drawers*, the quarterly publication of the University of South Carolina at Spartanburg, and in *Carolina Woman*. She has participated in readings in Spartanburg and in Graham, North Carolina.

Mrs. Williamson-Pratt comes from a family of writers—sister, niece, brother, daughter, and nephew. In her words, "Writing is an extension of the self. . .withheld from daily routine."

GROWING PAINS

You infuriate me with
your sullen silence
blank eyes focus
dead ahead and look
through me.

So quietly she left
I didn't know she was gone,
until I yelled
and the only response
was silence.

ALONE

It is the first night of Fall
in the year of obliqueness.
Veiny days drift endlessly
then join for the night of
swollen clots causing circles
to form life.
Much better it would be
if you were here...or...
where home used to be
when offspring knew what to expect,
incessant worry, fear, dread.
And now it is discovered that
that was love too,
a better love than not having
you to worry with.

BOOK REPORT

(To the Plaths of the World)

In time ahead
will you stand before pupils,
speak of struggles
discuss failures
contemplate insanity.

Will you say
she wrote confessionally,
in a bizarre fashion,
a style unique
for her time.

Will anyone remember
the words never recorded
which spoke her
tenderness.

TRAPS

Back when Daddy set traps
made from scrap lumber and
chicken wire,
I thought it cruel to
purposely plot to catch
the wild and free.

Now I think it cruel
for life to set traps
of steel.

HAIKU

Hair lifted on breeze
summer strands plied to moist lips
tastes of dried cotton.

HALLS OF JUSTICE

Curly haired child
dropping peanuts into Cheerwine,
blasé of your fate being meted
by gray haired lawyer in a
cold stone lobby.
Privacy denied you
by illiteracy,
speeches ring of justice
taking away your mother,
deciding her competency.

Simple it was,
so easy to take the
mother's rights away,
shake hands and agree
that we meters of law
did what was "best."

DEMOCRACY

The beautiful procession
crawled down Main Street
honoring a memory.
Shiny, sleek black sedans
of late model on parade.
I stare and wonder how
you can afford to transport
yourself in such finery.

Jaw bones tighten
muscles twitch as I
remember where I saw you
in another procession,
standing in the
Food Stamp Line.

RUSSIAN ROULETTE

On a firing squad line
you play Russian Roulette
with me
squeezing, releasing.
I squirm,
catapult to the edge of
saneness as your steel gray
eyes bore holes through my
inabilities.

FROSTBITE

Stifled of being me
yet who am I?
How can I know when
you own most of me?
I'm like a flower
bitten by frost.
I long to bloom
but find my petals
gone.

CAUCASIAN BIGOTRY

With Caucasian bigotry
I look at you and expect
black eyed peas to
spout from your mouth
as you "yes'm" my command
through fatback swollen lips.

I withdraw from your
cotton field stench
as you bend to tie my shoe.
I recoil when your chickory
hand brushes my foot and

I wonder how you got
stuck in that jelly jar
and why the KKK wastes time
on tarnished colored beings
and how mammies had babies
small enough to sit on
dime store candy counters.

Dumbly you hum snatches
of "Old Black Joe" as
"Oh Black Betty, Bam a Lam"
blares on sonic waves.

I ponder why Martin Luther
had so many brothers
and Alex Haley wasn't
satisfied to leave his
roots be.

Your blackness engulfs as
you rise from being
slave to the Master and
I cringe with shame at all
you overcame. . .
at burdens still heavy
on your shoulders.

You shuffle to your post
ignoring me as mature
mascara tears stream
for I had conveniently forgotten
my beloved Nanny.

IT WILL KEEP

Don't you realize that
I am new to this. . .
this being that I love you
but cannot break through
the walls you have built
about yourself.
I know you love me
but it's a painful love for you.
When you're ready you'll accept
my love. . .I cannot force you.
Why are you waiting,
holding back while we both
suffer loneliness and a deep
need of another who knows that,
as Sandburg said, "Love is a
deep and a dark and a lonely"
and it is.
So much so that my love for you
appears to me as a long black tunnel
where I stand waiting, hoping to catch
a glimmer.
As it is I see no end but my heart
imagines shades of gray penetrating
the blackness.
There are no fairy tales, my love,
we had ours when first we met,
when harbor lights and fishing fleets
sailed by full moonlight, and we battled
each one and they captured us not.
Breakers teased our toes
crashed about our sandy legs
currents pulled. . .pulled. . .
sucked at us
but our togetherness was too much
for a mere sea.
We stumbled and peeked through
swaying seaweed, laughing at
retreating vessels.
Our laughter ceased as we lay

sandy, wet, vulnerable,
ready for sharing more than
second childhood games.
By day you retracted
crab-like to the vise in which
you felt safe.
And I, the threat, still need you
to fulfill my fruits of
womanhood.

DREAMS

I wake from sleep pricked by
nails of your memory
driven deep into cells which
pump vital existence.
Blistered tears play the
corners of eyes which,
in total darkness,
see the lines of your grin-
creased mouth that pressed
mine on frost bitten mornings,
seeing eye fingers explore
the length of my body as we lay
encased in lovers' warmth.
Radiating sparks spread liquid
fire, singeing ruffled sheets.
Still, quite still I lie
as fear sweat breaks my pores,
I lie here. . .damp with memory.

LISTS

Decided to make a list,
very American of me,
methodical, organized.
Telltale black and white
of improvements long overdue.
Should I use Pros and Cons
or
Assets and Liabilities?
My pen flows with liabilities
and contemplating,
my ass sets.

ECOLOGY

How many are we who
smother the lands,
usurp natural wonders and
replace them with memory tours.
What kind of humans are we
who deface living
with crippling progress.

Tarred land, slain trees,
our mirth rings ridiculously
as a lone buttercup
peaks through pavement.

Far away the Milky Way
glitters with laughter
winks knowingly as,
seconds away,
the Ozone creeps.

POEIR
Under The